Frederick Boyle

A Ride Across a Continent

A Personal Narrative of Wanderings Through Nicaragua and Costa Rica (Volume 1)

Frederick Boyle

A Ride Across a Continent
A Personal Narrative of Wanderings Through Nicaragua and Costa Rica (Volume 1)

ISBN/EAN: 9783744745291

Printed in Europe, USA, Canada, Australia, Japan

Cover: Foto ©Andreas Hilbeck / pixelio.de

More available books at **www.hansebooks.com**

A RIDE ACROSS A CONTINENT:

A PERSONAL NARRATIVE OF WANDERINGS THROUGH
NICARAGUA AND COSTA RICA.

BY

FREDERICK BOYLE, F.R.G.S.,
AUTHOR OF "ADVENTURES AMONG THE DYAKS OF BORNEO."

IN TWO VOLUMES.

VOLUME I.

LONDON:
RICHARD BENTLEY, 8, NEW BURLINGTON STREET,
Publisher in Ordinary to Her Majesty.
1868.

THIS LIGHT NARRATIVE

OF HAPPY DAYS PASSED TOGETHER,

IN JUNGLE, AND MOUNTAIN, AND RIVER,

IS

DEDICATED

TO

JOHN GLADWYN JEBB,

THE DEAR FRIEND OF MY BOYHOOD,

OF MY MANHOOD,

AND, I TRUST, OF MY OLD AGE.

PREFACE.

The main object of the travels narrated in this book was to examine the antiquities of Nicaragua. Upon this ground no word of preface is needful, as the information we gathered on the early history of the country will be found in the body of my narrative; but some brief explanation of the "Rio Frio mystery," which we had hoped, and still hope, to solve, is necessary for the understanding of allusions and traditions in every part of the book.

Very few persons here, or even across the Atlantic, have heard of that secluded land in which a certain tribe of Costa Rican Indians have preserved their freedom, not unmolested, but never infringed, since the times of the discovery. New York papers, indeed, have once or twice given a short article on the (supposed) character of the country, and the (supposed) condition of the people; but as nothing whatever is known on these points, the conjectures of the journalist have necessarily been vague to an unusual degree.

We had hoped that before this work was published our renewed exploration might have filled another blank in the map of America; but, seeing no likelihood of immediate action, we have decided to put before the world these volumes, in hopes that the interest of travellers may be roused to aid our future exertions. The objections to owning a partial failure are, of course, very evident, but the indication of them may safely be left to the critics; and if this light work should call to our aid a few hardy fellows, endued with some slight faith in Pantagruelism, it will have answered our best purpose, and will more than atone for any slight regret one may feel in confessing a disappointment caused, we hope, by no want of energy on our own part.

It may perhaps be worth while, as illustrating a subject of which very, very little is known in England, to transcribe here a brief abstract from a paper read by the Author to the Ethnological Society, on the 11th of June last year. I see with the utmost plainness that an hypercritical critic may accuse me of false art in putting an immense head to a body supremely small; but disregarding this, in consideration of the great interest which, I find, the subject possesses to most minds, I venture to enter at some length into the question of the "bravo" tribes of Central America. "There are few persons in Europe, excepting such as have made this country a special study, who have any definite knowledge of the present condition of its Indian races. Some, I find, have a curiously vague idea that the Spaniards utterly destroyed the native population; others, that intermarriage, debauchery, and other plagues, which, as we are mysteriously told, invariably afflict a lower grade of human beings when confronted with the higher, have long since exterminated the pure Indian stock; others again, of superior information, believe that the aboriginal races were all reduced by their invaders, and remain as a docile working class unto this day. The latter impression is certainly true of three-fourths of them, or, at least, was so until ceaseless contests between whites and mestizos taught the coloured peon his overwhelming power, and here or there aroused his ambition and long latent ferocity. Of these 'Indios manzos,' or tame Indians, I do not design to speak; though very numerous in Guatemala, Honduras, and Nicaragua, they are, as yet, of little account politically, and the outbursts of their fury have not hitherto been followed by any definite assumption of power. Even Rafael Carrera, though for twenty years President and Dictator of Guatemala, governed by the hands of whites or mestizos; nor did the Indian 'peons,' who had raised their kinsman to power, ever attempt to claim authority in the republic.

"But in the nominal territory of the five states are many districts of various extent which have now no regard whatever for the white authority. Of some of these the inhabitants seem never to have been brought into contact with the Spanish power, and are to this day ignorant or careless of the white man's presence; such are the Menchés in Guatemala, a few tribes of Northern Mosquito, and the Pranzos, or Guatusos, of Costa Rica. Other races there are, probably more numerous, which resumed their independence after a period of subjection more or less prolonged. Among these may be noted the famous Indians of Darien and of Santa Catarina, visited by Scherzer and Von Tempsky. Beginning at Panama and travelling northward, I will very briefly enumerate the various tribes now absolutely or practically independent.

"First in order come the Indians of the isthmus, Darien, San Blas, and Mandinga, upon whom Dr. Cullen read an interesting paper last month to this Society. That gentleman asserts that the invaders never overcame these tribes; and although this fact seems doubtful to me, it is certain that at this day they regard Spaniards with the bitterest hatred. To English and Americans they are not quite so hostile, but every one must remember the disastrous explorations of Com. Prevost, R.N., and Lieutenant Strain of the United States Navy, in this terrritory.

"Northward of these, in the tract disputed by New Granada and Costa Rica, — every boundary of Central America is a casus belli ever present—lie the Talamancas, who extend as far as the bay of Matina. These Indians are said to be numerous, and the people of Costa Rica declare them to be allied in race with the Guatusos, but they are not nearly so ferocious. As I was told in San José, it is no unusual event for an adventurous young trader to lead a mule or two into their country, where, if he be not murdered, he will make an enormous profit. The Talamancas live as agriculturists, and are in no way dangerous if not disturbed.

"Northward of these again are the far-famed Guatusos, or Pranzos, who inhabit a territory lying between the Merivales mountains on the west, the lake of Nicaragua and the San Juan river on the north, the Atlantic shore on the east, and the table-land of San José upon the south. Of this tribe I shall speak more at length.

"Across the San Juan river, in the republic of Nicaragua, and the reservation of Mosquito, are very numerous tribes, Woolwas, Moscas, Ramas, Poyas, Towkas, Xicaques, and Caribs. The population of these tribes is quite unknown, estimates varying from 8000 to 25,000. They seem all to be quite savage, although practising many of the virtues belonging to a more civilised existence, such as cleanliness, and industry, and chastity. It is probable that they have neither advanced nor fallen back in their condition since the time of the conquest; but on the other hand it must be owned that the Moscas have degenerated vastly in that martial spirit which so frequently routed the valour of the Spaniards.

"To the north-west of Nicaragua lies San Salvador, which alone of Central American states has no hostile population of Indians. 'There is, nevertheless,' says Mr. Squier, 'a portion of this state where the aborigines have always maintained an almost complete isolation, and where they still retain their original manners, and to a great extent their ancient rites and ceremonies.' This district is known as the Costa del Balsimo, or Balsam Coast. It is about fifty miles long by twenty to twenty-five broad, lying between La Libertad, the port of San Salvador, and the roadstead of Acajutla, near Sonsonate. This district is entirely occupied by Indians, retaining habits but little changed from what they were at the time of the conquest. It is only traversed by footpaths, so intricate and difficult as to baffle the efforts of the stranger to penetrate its recesses. The difficulty of intercourse is enhanced, if not by the actual hostility of the natives, by their dislike to any intrusion on the part of the whites, be they Spaniards or foreigners. These people are called Nahuals, and are thought, with some probability, to be Aztec in origin, and allied to the Niquirans of Nicaragua.

"Northward of San Salvador, and stretching from sea to sea, lies Guatemala, the most powerful of the five republics. Its nominal territory is vastly curtailed by Indian tribes partly or wholly ignoring the central authority. The most powerful of those which have never been subdued are the Menchés, inhabiting the north-eastern corner of the state. So spirited and hostile are these people, that in 1837 the then Government of Central America found it necessary to make a league of friendship with their Cacique. In this document all pretensions of authority over them were yielded,—which was indeed no great privation to the whites, seeing that not one had ever ventured into their territory. Also, certain stipulations were made providing the free passage of missionaries ' to instruct the young Indians in civilised knowledge;' but such have been the disturbances of the republic, that no effort has been made to profit by this permit,—which is probably fortunate for the missionaries, and not quite unlucky for the Menchés.

Of another race of Indians, virtually free, and most jealous of strangers, Von Tempsky gives an interesting account in ' Mitla.' They live almost due north of Quesaltenango, and their numbers are estimated at 24,000 souls. Except in that they have adopted a drunken parody of Christianity, with which they relieve the monotony of human sacrifice, these people, said to be Quiché by race, preserve all the customs of their forefathers before the Spanish conquest. I may add, that those customs, with the exception of the sacrifices aforesaid, seem to be quite as civilised, much more decent, and infinitely more orderly than those of the surrounding Christians.

" In the north of Vera Paz, to the west of

Peten, and all along the Usumacinta, dwell numerous and warlike tribes, called generally Lacandones. They are of one stock with the Menchés, of whom I have before spoken. It is of course quite impossible to estimate the power of these races, their civilization, or customs, but I may observe that all Guatemalans agree in assigning 100,000 souls to the Menché race alone; and not a few have assured me that the Lacandones generally are more numerous than all the remaining population of the republic. This would give them something like 900,000 souls, but it is mere guesswork and tradition. That they are very numerous is beyond doubt, for until the middle of the last century they kept the whole northern part of Guatemala in continual terror by their fierce incursions. Certainly the Lacandones and their country, so mysterious and romantic, offer one of the most interesting subjects of exploration left in the world. Whether or no we believe in the Itzimaya, the great city of golden mystery, we must at least feel a thrill of excitement in reflecting that a territory exists in which such a romance is possible. That the Itzis or Lacandones were very highly civilised only one hundred and fifty years ago, we are assured by the report of Mazariegos, who captured their island city of Flores, in 1695. Valenzuela, who accompanied the invading forces, and took part in their barbarous destruction of palaces and temples, tells us that the Indian buildings were far handsomer and more solidly built than those of Guatemala. Fleeing from Peten into the wilderness, the Lacandones disappeared from view, and it may be they raised again in Vera Paz the stately edifices which Spanish Vandals had destroyed. Waldeck observes, that certain of these Indians whom he met were dressed in the precise fashion of the Palenque monuments. Any gentleman who has seen a picture of those monuments will readily believe that they cut a peculiarly curious figure.

"Into Mexico proper I do not design to enter.

"In the eastern and northern parts of Honduras, the departments of Yoro and Olancho, are several 'bravo' tribes—Payas, Secos, Xicaques, and Caribs. None of these have ever been conquered, except the latter, who, as every one knows, were deported from Saint Vincent by the English. The most noticeable peculiarity known of these Indians is their custom of living all together in one house, like the Dyaks of Borneo. Each family has an apartment of its own. They are peaceful, industrious, and remarkably cleanly. Under ordinary circumstances they are friendly with the white population, but they absolutely decline to submit to the authority of the Republic.

" Of Yucatan I have not been able to obtain any reliable information. Stephens observes that there *may be* ' bravo' Indians in the interior, of which very little is known, but he does not assert that he was absolutely so informed. If this be so, we should expect to find them in a condition much more advanced than the other unconquered tribes, excepting the Lacandones, for the Mayas of Yucatan were, and still are very superior in intelligence to the other Indians of Central America."

Of all these independent tribes, the Guatusos should be most interesting to English travellers. The broad San Juan river, which now, subject to protest, forms the boundary between Nicaragua and Costa Rica, has two large tributaries descending from the Merivalles and the San José table-land; the most easterly, that is, nearest the Atlantic, is the Serebpiqui, of which the reader will hear more; next, the San Carlos. Both of these are rocky, mountainous streams, full of rapids, and subject to dangerous floods; little adapted, in fact, for transport purposes. But there is a third river, larger than the easterly streams, which falls into the Lake of Nicaragua almost at the point in which the San Juan flows out of it. So far as any one has had courage to explore, it is a slow, deep stream, much blocked with fallen timber, but in other respects suited for navigation. This is the mysterious Frio. Where its waters rise, their course, and the dangers of the stream, are points utterly unknown. One fact alone is sure about the Frio— that its head-waters are the favourite haunt or habitation of the Guatusos. The growing commerce of Costa Rica has striven hard for an outlet on the Atlantic shore, and bold woodsmen have at various times cut a mule-track through the forest to the Serebpiqui and San Carlos; but the dangers of navigation in these streams are too great for commerce. The Rio Frio is that outlet provided by Nature for the produce of San José coffee grounds; but Nature had to provide for her Indian children also, and she posted the Guatuso family upon this San José canal.

Everything connected with that fierce race is enveloped in awful mystery; but it is curious that all accounts agree in giving them an origin far from their present seats. The story current in Costa Rica cannot fail to interest the Englishman, even if he be not converted to a belief in its truth. When Sir Francis Drake retired to the Pacific shore, after the sack of Esparsa, say they, a large body of his men mutinied, in mad hopes of holding that town against the Creole forces, and resting peaceably there. Drake left them to their fate. But when the Spanish army assembled, and the mutineers found themselves nearly surrounded, they hastily retired through the forests of the Merivalles, with the intention of cutting their way to the friendly Mosquito shore. Unquestionably this route would lead through the country of the modern Guatusos, who were then called "Pranzos." It is certain that the buccaneers never crossed the San Juan, and equally certain that the Spaniards never fell in with them: many believe that, wearied out with hardships, they settled round the headwaters of the Frio, destroying the male population, and taking the women to wife. The universal legend of the surrounding peoples—Indians, Caribs, Nicaraguans, and Costa Ricans,—declares the Guatuso race to be distinguished by fair hair and blue eyes.* It is not a little curious that in the various fights and defeats of invading expeditions an Indian has scarcely ever been seen by any reliable witness; the arrow whizzes from the hand of an unseen archer, the celt strikes silently from behind.† Costa Ricans say that the buccaneer blood so changed the Indian complexion that the Pranzos gained their new

* Of course I vouch nothing for these legends, which could only be verified by very complete exploration. For my own part I do not believe the Guatusos are white, in our sense of the word; at least at the present day. M. Frœbel gives a romantic story of a young German who fell into their hands—was tied to a tree—awful tortures—chief's daughter—put her arms round him—touching speech—saved his life—married her—and all that; but the German, who is now leading a civilized life near San Francisco, says nothing about the white colour.

† Of these disastrous expeditions I have outlined the principal in my narrative. Captain Parker, who, with three French friends, went some little way up the river, shot an Indian, whose colour " was about that of a Comanche." This would certainly be different from the usual complexion, but decidedly not very fair. His hair was long and black.

name, "Guatusos," or red rabbits, from the colour of their hair and the fairness of their complexion. Such is the Costa Rican tradition, which is so strongly accredited there, that an European minister, forgetful of chronology, fervently prayed us to carry a union jack in front of our exploring party. Another story referring to the same event describes the fugitives as tame Indians, who took advantage of the buccaneer disturbances to make their escape over the mountains. In Nicaragua, various stories, more or less improbable, are current. Some assert that in a grand foray, the Guatusos, who came from Mosquito, carried off thousands of Spanish women, whereby the natural complexion was changed. In reference to this theory, one must needs inquire where on earth the women came from? All Nicaragua would not have given tens for the thousands needed. Others believe the Guatusos to be descended from the old inhabitants of Zapatero, who fled from that island in a single night, scared by the practice of Christianity as shown by missionary padres. Possibly there is truth in all these stories, and the population of the Rio Frio is made up from the bravest fragments of many surrounding tribes.

In regard to their condition, nothing whatever is reliably known. Padre Zepeda, a Jesuit, declared in 1750 that he lived many months among them, and was kindly entertained. He speaks of towns and houses and gardens. The latter point is certainly curious, if the padre really meant to describe a garden as we understand the word. His report caused several missionary expeditions to be despatched up the Frio and over the mountains, but the Guatusos were found to be quite as ready to despatch missionaries as the most zealous bishop could be. And so these attempts were gradually abandoned, with no further success than the addition of several martyrs to the calendar; nevertheless, some of these parties approached the Indian territory so as to see towns, and immense fields under cultivation.

Independently of romance, the exploration of the Rio Frio is of great importance to civilisation. The richest specimens of gold quartz I ever saw came from this district, and the weirdly fame of the Guatusos, who act as dragons watching treasure, alone deters a swarm of adventurous diggers from hastening there. Lying as it does between the San Juan river, the Atlantic, and the coffee grounds of Costa Rica, it is evident that if a railroad or canal should ever be carried across Nicaragua, a branch line, or at least a solid road, must be constructed along the banks of the Frio, to convey the growing commerce of San José. Sooner or later then the Guatusos *must* be disturbed, for it would be preposterous to retain the present trade route by Punt 'Arenas, Panama, or the Horn, if any lasting transit scheme were opened in Nicaragua. Such a branch line would revolutionize the whole trade of Costa Rica, which has now no communication with the Atlantic coast.

The three principal attempts at exploration that have been made in modern times will be found related at length in my narrative.

Finally, all portable antiquities mentioned in this book are now in the British Museum.

One word to the critics. Some time since I published a book of travels upon Borneo, and certainly I had no cause to complain of unkindness on the part of any reviewer of that work. But there were a few papers which gently but firmly called me to order for "levity" and a "habit of sneering." Nothing could be further from my wish at any time. There *are* absurdities in the world, or at least so it seems to some of us, at which we had best laugh; but laughter and "sneering" are very different, and in some sort opposite to one another. If I have sinned again in this book, I beg pardon from amalgamated virtue, and protest I never meant it; but I won't promise not to do so again. I have striven to make my works amusing; if they be instructive also, why, so much the better! But pray accuse me not of failing to do what I never attempted. After all, "Le style c'est l'homme;" and no earthly permission is needed for a man to be what he is.

Paris, July 14, 1866.

ILLUSTRATIONS.

Foot of the Lake Road, Masaya . *Frontispiece*, Vol. I.
Nicaraguan Sculpture . . . . Page 161, Vol. I.

Meeting of Travellers in Nicaragua *Frontispiece*, Vol. II.
Sepulchral Statuary of Nicaragua . . Page 43, Vol. II.
Ancient Pottery from Nicaragua . . Page 96, Vol. II.

CONTENTS OF VOLUME I.

CHAPTER I.

Our party—St. Thomas—Kingston—Aspinwall—First view of Greytown—Greytown bar—Landing—Our hotel—American acquaintances—The lagoon—Captain P—— —A Rio Frio story—Our Colorado picnic—Droll scenes—The Colorado—Rumours of marvels—Heroism of the filibusters—Scenes on board and on the bank—The "tuboba"—Scarlet frogs—Venomous lizards—Return to Greytown . . . 1

CHAPTER II.

Californian Transit Company—The "Old Transit"—Captain Pim's scheme—The Governor of Greytown—Story of a Rio Frio expedition—Kidnapping a British subject—The river San Juan—Story of Mr. S—— —His domestic arrangements—Castillo Viejo—Rapids—San Carlos—Condition of the people—Mouth of the Frio river—Lake of Nicaragua—Ometepec—Zapatero—Indian reservations—Filibusters—Granada—Houses and customs—Hotel—Presidio—Churches—Siege and assault of the filibusters—Revolutions—Amusements—Scorpions—Hammock-living 33

CHAPTER III.

Ellis's strange malady—Ascent of Mombacho—Start for Chontales—First camp—Catching an alligator—Booted and barefoot classes in Nicaragua—Geographical problem—A long forest ride—Shooting one's supper—Lassoing a bull—Nicaraguan roads—Casa Blanca—A tropical stream—Juigalpa—Amiable priest—Indian remains—Tomb-breaking—Tales of mystery—Uncanny behaviour of our Indian host—More tales of wonder—Great tombs—Portrait statues—Restoration—A dreary camp—Pumas—Catching a puma—A weary night—Garrapatas—Arrival at Libertad 105

CHAPTER IV.

The gold country of Libertad—Wandering diggers—Crowded lodgings—Mr. D——'s bed—Gold-mining—Tomb-breaking on a large scale—Corale snake—The find—The second cairn—Country round Libertad—Idols—Amusements—We give a ball—The national dance—Wonderful exhibitions of devotion— Christmas Day at the diggings—Other Christmas Days A narrow escape—Days of excitement—Reflections upon the fine old massacre of former times—Kind warnings from the women—Another Frio Story—The final challenge—Leave Libertad—A mighty bird—Cannibal fish—An alligator's walk—Colossal head—Advice to future antiquarians—A long ride—A pleasant camp—An opinion about the canal scheme. 179

CHAPTER V.

ROUGH SKETCH OF NICARAGUA AT THE CONQUEST.

Arrival of Gil Gonsalez de Avila—Mexican empire in Nicaragua—Curious historical fact—The great cacique Nicaragua—Shrewd questions—Hostile Chiefs—Fortune of Gonsalez—Appointment of Hernandez de Cordova to be governor—Invasion of the country by Gonsalez—Treachery—Pleasant scouting—Murder of Ch. de Olid—Murder of Hernandez—Forgery of Contreras—Murder of Valdiviesso—Amazing scheme of Ferdinand de Contreras—His death—Languages of Nicaragua—Ancient races—Civilization—Various Customs—Religion — Sacrifices — Oppression of the Indians — Two opinions about these things—Where are the Chontals now?—Customs of the Woolwas at the present day—Muros—Carcas—Devineos—Glorious remains on the banks of the Mico—An appeal to antiquarians 250

A RIDE ACROSS A CONTINENT.

CHAPTER I.

Our party—St. Thomas—Kingston—Aspinwall—First view of Greytown—Greytown bar—Landing—Our hotel—American acquaintances—The lagoon—Captain P――.—A Rio Frio story—Our Colorado picnic—Droll scenes—The Colorado—Rumours of marvels—Heroism of the filibusters—Scenes on board and on the bank—The "tuboba"—Scarlet frogs—Venomous lizards—Return to Greytown.

On the 17th of October, 1865, we took passage for Greytown, on the Royal Mail Steam-ship "Shannon." Our party consisted of Mr. Jebb, myself, Mr. J. D――, secretary, and an English groom, Ellis: our objects I have explained in the preface. The ocean behaved becomingly to us, our fellow-passengers were pleasant, and so soon as all on board had become duly impressed with the importance of the position held in this world by the captain of a Royal Mail Packet, everything passed agreeably.

The news of the Morant Bay insurrection reached us at St. Thomas. That little green island, upon which the red and white town seems so curiously to climb, was in a great ferment; and, indeed, if the sentiments of two boatmen, who rowed us about the harbour, showed truly the desires generally entertained by the negro population, with reason enough were the residents alarmed. These two fellows, one of whom was black and the other coloured, informed us that the people of Jamaica had behaved in the most virtuous manner, and hinted that the overwhelming number of whites in the other islands alone preserved them from a similar fate. This, it should be remembered, was before the news of the suppression had reached St. Thomas, or, at least, before its details were credited by the blacks. Of course, no one in his senses will justify certain passages in the conduct of the military at Jamaica; but if such ideas were abroad in the West Indian islands—and very few dispute this fact—here is surely some justification for Governor Eyre and the other authorities.

From St. Thomas we ran to Kingston, where those who love such sights might have beheld seven negroes hanging on one tree about five miles from the town; so at least we were assured, but very probably it was not true. One of our fellow-passengers escaped narrowly. He had just succeeded to an estate at Morant Bay, and was going to inspect his property. The name of a friend in the neighbourhood, who had invited him to be his guest, was first on the list of murdered which reached us at St. Thomas.

At Kingston we saw the commanding officer —Colonel Fyfe, I think—a sergeant, and several men, belonging to the Maroon Volunteer Corps, of which such extraordinary stories have been told in England. We found the sergeant a very civil, respectable man, and the privates as well dressed and as decent-looking as any others of the negro population. The sergeant was carefully carrying a "fetish," picked up after the rout of the negroes: it was merely a rude wooden figure, about eighteen inches high, wound about with blue riband and feathers. Why do all dark races relapse into idolatry the moment they break with the European power? Is it possible they regard Christianity as essentially a portion of the white yoke, to be outwardly revered and copied, like the rest of his law, so long as his power endures, but to be thrown on one side at the first movement of independence? Whatever be the cause, it may, I think, be safely asserted that every converted race of dark skin has returned to its native superstition when a blow for freedom was to be struck against the white sovereignty. Of this I shall be enabled to give a very curious proof in the course of my narrative.

The decay of Kingston has been too much commented on of late to require remark from me. The silent and dusty streets, the rotting houses, the wretched appearance of the negroes, when contrasted with the state of those islands in the possession of foreign nations, tell a tale of ill-informed benevolence, and of weak and shuffling government, too often repeated under our balanced system. Could we import Chinamen by wholesale, as the French did, and abandon the traffic with stern condemnation when our object was gained, we might restore our West Indies to something of their former splendour; but such a course is impossible. Our lovely islands must rot under the incubus.

From Kingston to Aspinwall, where we had the most distressful partings possible, was the next stage. Oh, that dreadful day in Colon, when the last glimmer of the blue dresses had been whirled from our sight, and nothing remained for us but to wander on the wharf and survey the long range of " bars " and billiard-rooms which compose the town!

Twenty-four hours more brought us to Greytown, or San Juan del Norté, as the Nicaraguans call it. When we came on deck in the early morning, the sky was dark and ragged, a cold wind blew from shore, the sea was rough and muddy. Before us lay a low, dull, swampy coast, and as far as the eye could reach stretched a dusky green plain, unbroken by any hill or visible river. Over a long stretch of bare sand was a misty line of timber-built houses painted white, close behind which rose the dark forest wall. Three weatherbeaten palms stood all solitary at the end of a naked sandspit, and at their feet lay an overturned canoe and a skeleton tree washed up by the waves. A swampy village, a dreary and a desolate, Greytown appeared, as we lay off in the "Ruahine," and waited for the Carib canoes.

Before leaving the vessel we issued invitations for dinner on the following day to every officer off duty, but not a solitary acceptance did we obtain. Once on a time, two gentlemen belonging to the Royal Mail Service went ashore at Greytown, and the report they gave on returning aboard diffused such universal panic, that no officer has since ventured to leave his vessel while off the Nicaraguan coast. Finding all temptation to be utterly vain before this well-grounded horror, we embarked alone in a cargo-boat, pursued by a tearful chorus of advice and sympathy. By great good fortune the sea had become tolerably smooth, and we crossed the bar without further accident than wet knees and a teetotum-like revolution of our boat. Mischance is terribly common in this shark-haunted surf. For the conveyance of the mails, Mr. Paton, the English Consul, has a crew of Caribs* specially engaged, for no other race of men could

---

* Whatever the Caribs may have been when first deported from St. Vincent, they are now negroes in every respect, excepting that they show an industry and perseverance rarely met with in the African character. The mahogany cutting is entirely in their hands, and as

perform this perilous duty with the punctuality required. No serious accident has yet happened to these bold surf-men, but the mail-bags are generally dripping when landed.

Inside the sandspit which is forming across the channel, the canoe glides along a vast meadow of water-grass, over beds of aquatic flowers and long tangles of purple blossom. On every side are the pretty red and yellow birds called spurwings, which hover and flutter above the water like butterflies, with wings vertically upraised, and sink at length among the weed with a coo of contentment. Big white cranes flap heavily seaward, disturbed in their reedy haunts by the rustle of our canoe; and flocks of awkward needle-ducks skim over the water, or sit with wings outstretched upon a floating log. There is little picturesque beauty in the harbour of Greytown; one feels oppressed with odours of the swamp, and a prevailing sense of flatness. Everything is so level, so damp, so green.

---

boatmen they only yield to the Mosquito Indians, whose regular services cannot be obtained. It is gratifying to notice the invariable enthusiasm with which all the inhabitants of the Atlantic coast speak of the Caribs.

Presently we came upon a few palm trees and a few wooden shanties. Then we encountered a gentlemanly old Spaniard in his shirt-sleeves, standing upon a rotten log half buried in oozy swamp grass. This personage, our crew assured us, was the Carib Consul, placed at the entrance of the town to prevent the importation of oil extracted from mosquitoes, now much manufactured in England. Native industry required fostering. After an interchange of friendly advice, we left this individual standing on his log. More wooden shanties, more water-puddles, more damp grass; then a rotting wooden jetty in front of a shed proclaimed to be the " Royal Mail Steam-ship Company's Wharf and Warehouse." Here we shipped our oars, for the heart of the town was reached.

Upon the rotten wharf was a tiny little coloured boy, very clean, and neat, and—self-possessed, let us say, as most coloured boys are, especially tiny ones. Upon seeing us he produced an enormous pencil and a note-book of corresponding dimensions. As the cargo was lifted out of our boat, he made entries of great magnitude in the large note-book: the clerk of the Royal Mail Steam-ship Company was before us. "Say! Cap'n Simon," says he, to an honest-looking black man, unloading the boat, " Say ! Cap'n Simon ! Hev ye heard the news ? The black folks at Jamaica hev ris'n and killed all the white *and* COLOURED folks; they blank black niggers air no good on airth, *I* say. They be blank !" "Eh, mus'r ! and whatta they do that for ?" "They blank blank 'say! They want all the land to theirselves. It's all 'long of the missionaries. They ain't no 'count at all, they missionaries ; they're at the handle-end of all mischief. They ain't no 'count at all—blank !"

Here "Cap'n" Simon pulled him up short by questioning the accuracy of his "ile" account, and we left the little yellow Solon among the paint cans. It was amusing to us subsequently to hear the Jamaica negroes of Greytown discussing this revolt. The devoted loyalty of their expressions was quite touching; let us hope it was also sincere. In the West Indies a negro, or a nigger, is a black man born in Africa; all those born in the colony call themselves Creoles, like white people. The negroes, who, in fact, compose almost the whole population of Greytown, are a quiet and comparatively industrious body; but with prosperity care has come, and the chuckling "yap-yap" of laughter, which resounds so pleasantly in the island towns, is seldom heard here. The negroes laugh like other people, and are no fun at all.

If eight hundred travellers descend upon a village of seven hundred inhabitants, and stay there ten days, what will be the awful result? Not eight hundred virtuous artisans, each provided with a paper of sandwiches, and a bottle of beer in a side pocket, but eight hundred wild Californians, all nuggets and bowie knives, each one of whom is bound to have three meals a-day, and liquor whenever he—something—pleases? Our Greytown experience enables us to answer this question. The town on which such fate shall fall will be sacked as by an army of Huns; and succeeding travellers, passing through on their lawful business, shall be exposed without redress to the extremes of hunger and thirst; since for all landladylike shortcomings an excuse exists against the force of which cavil must impotently break: "Three days ago, sir, we had eight hundred Californians here on the Transit, and they stayed ten days. We had fifty of them in this house." Fifty of them in the Union Hotel! Fifty elephants in a loose box! This building, in which we took up our quarters, was twenty feet in breadth by seventy feet in length, inclusive of a verandah and back kitchen. It was built of wood, as are all the houses of Greytown ; upon the ground floor was a bare flagged bar, a bare flagged dining-room, and a kitchen barer than either. On the upper floor were sixteen bedrooms, all of them more than six feet square. Leaving our baggage to be carried up, we strolled across a wet meadow to this hotel, and entered the bar; the landlord made his appearance, and introduced himself as Captain Fletcher. On his retirement to arrange our rooms, a gentleman with a weatherbeaten face and a thick moustache approached us, and said, with much cordiality—" Haow a'y you, gentlemen?" Then, after a moment's thought, he added triumphantly—" Naow *you*'ve come by the steamer"—as if he himself were in the habit of travelling by balloon. Having long since determined to conform in every respect to the native habits, we replied mildly that we had come by the steamer, and spat against a pillar, to show we were acquainted with American manners. This action seemed to strike our inquiring friend. He looked hard at the three lonely cocoa-palms upon the sandspit, glanced at us from the corner of his eye, and after a pause observed—" Kind o' dry this, ain't it?" In innocence we objected that the scene appeared to us rather damp. " Yes," he said. " Natur's damp here, but humans air always dry. Say! shall we take a drink?" Following the usages of the country, we took a drink, and the landlord and his barman kindly joined. Our hospitable acquaintance was then introduced as Captain Somebody, and the barman confided to me his own name, which was Joe.

Revolving many things in mind we retired to our rooms, which were clean and fresh and neat beyond our most luxurious expectations. On descent for dinner we found the bar-room crowded with Americans,[*] among whom were Captain P——, Captain Y——, Captain S——,

[*] It is strangely significant and prophetic that the Spanish inhabitants of the continent give the name of American exclusively to the people of the United States, who have unconsciously adopted the same habit in speaking of themselves.

and Captain W——. My companion was instantly saluted as Captain Jebb, while the landlord presented me all round as Captain Boyle. Nay, if my ear did not fail me, I heard our secretary addressed as Captain D——; and it was Ellis's own fault if he did not retain a military title suited to his ambition.

A very short stroll introduces the traveller to all that is to be seen of Greytown; and a very pretty little village it is—all white paint and green leaves and wavy palm trees. The streets are not paved with neck-breaking stones, nor cut out of the white and blinding sand as in other Central American towns, but are covered with turf as verdant as an English lawn. In the midst of the village is a large green, which would remind the wanderer of many a pleasant old-fashioned scene at home, were it not for the feathery cocoa-palms planted at intervals along the grass. On the land side of the houses are meadows and wild gardens, separated from the jungle by canal-like lagoons, which were filled at that time of the year to a considerable depth. For we had arrived in an unusually wet season, and November is always a watery month at

Greytown. Within an hour of our landing, the rain began to descend in such a manner that the "John Crows" were in danger of drowning in mid air, and any disbeliever in the Biblical deluge must have been converted on the instant. Along this Atlantic coast the climate is frequently irregular; the dry and rainy seasons are sometimes almost transposed. Floods are excessively common. In the terrific hurricane which swept down Blewfields river, a short time previous to our arrival, an island was washed away bodily, carrying with it eleven persons, whose bodies were never recovered. Fever and ague, that curse of the Tropics, is very prevalent; but I am satisfied that the excessive mortality of Greytown is to be attributed to the habits of the people rather than to any unhealthiness of the climate. If that remark, ever ringing in one's ears about the American barrooms—"Wal! this is the dryest party ever I see. Say! shall we take a drink?"—were less uttered or less frequently applauded, the Transit Company would not suffer such an annual loss of men, nor the climate of Nicaragua be so badly reputed.

Behind the village is a large lagoon, which winds about for miles, sometimes narrowing to a mere canal, but finally stretching out into a broad sheet of water. The loveliness of this little lake, the brightness and variety of the foliage that walls it in and reflects itself in the clear, dark water, the silent beauty of its long vistas, defy description. A broad grassy border of the brightest green edges round the shallows; and from this verdant carpet a thousand strange varieties of aquatic plants spring into brilliant blossom. The dense tropical foliage droops heavily under the sunbeams, and dips its boughs in the shaded water. Tufted lianas hang like ropes from the trees, and sway gently with the stifled breeze. Here and there floats a huge alligator, showing the long ridge of his scaly back above the surface; big bullfrogs give forth a shuddering croak at slow intervals; a jungle crow wakes up with a drowsy cry and flits noiselessly over the water; or a startled lizard drops from his bough and scurries away without wetting a scale of his shining skin. Musically from the distance come the cries and laughter of bathing negro girls; the foam swirls and trickles beneath the light paddle; and we glide along in a lotus dream until our Carib boatman rouses us by a sudden burst of wild song.

The amusements of Greytown are not numerous, but in general scheme they resemble those of better-known latitudes. On the night of our arrival, positively the very first night, we were invited to a ball—a downright live dance —from which "ladies of colour" were excluded. And it was a success, too, for white ladies attended to the number of nine, and among them was an unmarried one. Besides such dissipations, which it must be admitted are not so frequent as might be wished, there are pigs, and wild ducks, and tapirs, and manetee, and panthers, and many other interesting beasts, all to be shot in the neighbourhood As for the pigs and the manetee, Greytown, from the stories of the residents, would seem to be suffering a plethora of them; but, though searching assiduously, none were to be found by us, and other strangers have we encountered who gave the same report. I mention the fact because it seems curious.

On the day after arrival, November 12, we

walked through a swampy meadow, among thickets of guava and sand apple, to the office of the Transit Company.* There we found Captain G——, the chief, and Captain P——, restoring the equilibrium of fluids, after the severity of the previous evening, with champagne cocktails. The latter of these gentlemen had been one of the most distinguished filibusters, and commanded the crack corps of Walker's army, the Nicaraguan Rangers. Certainly he presented the very ideal of a dashing soldier of fortune. Captain G—— told us numerous tales of "Indian fighting" in Texas and California, enlivening them with a more than common share of that grotesque wit so characteristic of the Western Americans. We stayed a long time at this house, fascinated by the odd drollery of our host's conversation, and finally accepted an invitation to join a surveying party starting in a few days for the mouth of the Colorado on Transit business.

The Rio Frio question was discussed in all its bearings; and Captain P——, as we understood, expressed a wish to join us as a volunteer if we should succeed in forming an expedition. Our

* Of this enterprise I speak in the following chapter.

intention had long been to give him absolute command over the discipline of the party in case we should have more Americans than English when our numbers were finally filled. For this abdication we had many reasons. Yankees are difficult to manage under the best circumstances; Western men are the most unruly among Yankees; and such reckless spirits as are the majority of the Greytownians it would be simply impossible to control except by the exhibition of an "outrecuidence" superior to their own. That P—— was the man for this post we had been assured before leaving England, and a personal acquaintance gave us great confidence in his capacity.

Besides, the river was to some extent known to him already. In 1864, in company with three Frenchmen, he ascended the Frio in a small canoe. For five days they mounted the stream, which narrowed gradually, and on the sixth came to a fork, apparently enclosing an extensive swamp. From time to time patches of cultivated plantain had been observed upon the banks, and rude huts similar to those in use among the Mosquito tribes; but up to the sixth

morning no other traces of man were seen
except a few of the curious little rafts on which
the Guatusos navigate these rapid streams with
such singular skill. Shortly after leaving this
fork, the daring explorers came to a sharp turn
in the river, which was here much obstructed
with timber and covered with weeds. On
swinging round the angle at a considerable pace,
they suddenly found themselves face to face with
a tall savage clothed in a panther skin, who
seemed to be spearing fish as he stood astride
upon his raft. The Indian scarcely lost presence
of mind for a moment. Throwing down the
spear he snatched up a bow, and drew the long
reed arrow to the head, pointing it at P——, who
sat in the bows of the canoe. P—— owned to
us that he felt paralysed for the moment. His
fate seemed hopeless. The Indian, whose dark
face looked devilish with fear and malignity,
was scarcely fifteen feet away; his bow was
drawn to the full stretch, and no earthly accident seemed able to prevent its discharge. But
for the hundredth time P——'s life was saved by
a chance. For some reason or other the Indian
did not seem to fancy the first arrow, and threw

it down, hastily drawing another from his quiver. In the very act, Robert, a Frenchman, shot him through the heart. He fell backwards into the water, and a strong eddy carried his body towards the canoe. P—— and the others all assert that his complexion was as dark as that of a Comanche, and indeed that he resembled those Indians in his cast of features. It is a universal belief along the Atlantic coast, from Belize to Aspinwall, that the Frio tribe have white complexions, fair hair, and grey eyes.

We subsequently made acquaintance with the three Frenchmen who were with P—— on this expedition, and they all admitted that they were "badly scared." In the hurried consultation held after the Indian's death, it was unanimously determined to turn back; for in such a situation none of the party cared to meet savages whose courage apparently was not to be shaken even by the sight of such strange objects as white men must have seemed to them. On a stream so narrow, and so thicky blocked with snags and timber, every man of the little party might at any moment be shot from the bank, or from cover of a log, without sight of his enemy; and that the Guatusos are tolerable marksmen former massacres had shown. Accordingly, the canoe was put about in all haste; and, their panic growing on them, they paddled unceasingly until reaching San Carlos at the mouth of the river. In seventeen hours, aided by the current, they had retraversed the distance previously accomplished in six days.

But we understood Captain P—— to say he was anxious to return, and take a more careful "prospect" of the gold-bearing Frio district, and would wish to volunteer into any party we might organize. That we should have misunderstood him upon this point was very unfortunate.

We spent the time until the start of the Colorado survey, in wandering about the woods and harbour, shooting various birds and beasts. On the appointed day we joined the party, and embarked on board a small steamer under the command of Captain P——. In the mean time we had made an addition to our numbers in the person of "Sammy," a white Creole boy from Jamaica, who entered our service as Spanish interpreter to Ellis, and for "general utility."

There were about twenty Americans on board besides the crew, and some few "Dutchmen," as Germans are indiscriminately called on the other side of the Atlantic. In a very few minutes we made out that our fellow-guests were of a type quite different from any hitherto encountered in all our wanderings. Tall, upright, broad-shouldered men they were nearly all. Their heads were well set on, hands and feet small, muscles like iron. Every movement was quick and decided: there seemed to be a restless activity about them which kept the deck in a continual bustle. Their language was a compound of extravagant humour and improbable blasphemy. Practical jokes, of which the Dutchmen were usually victims, went on everywhere, and six-foot filibusters rolled with laughter like children. We were among the very pick of the Western States—men highly thought of even there for reckless daring.

They were simply the most good-natured, good-tempered fellows I ever met with. Our previous knowledge of Texans and Missourians and Californians was confined to a general impression of humour, and ingenious swearing, and ever-present revolvers—an impression principally traced by a severe treatment of Mayne Reid's novels undergone at school. On finding the two former points of this description so thoroughly realised, we began to regard the construction of the rifles and pistols strewn about the deck with no slight interest. There were one or two instruments of abnormal shape, which would, I am confident, have caused novel sensations in the most hardened frame; but not a single specimen could we see which comforted us by a won't-go-off appearance; they all looked painfully wicked. But to speak seriously, there was no possibility of anything disagreeable. That nineteen out of twenty Americans on board would have shot a man with just the same indifference as I should feel in shooting a monkey, is probably true enough—the greater part had long since "fait leur epreuves" in that respect—but bad temper we never met with among these wild fellows. The Western man will bear any amount of rough jesting from an acquaintance, or even from a stranger if he be a "right bhoy;" and the joke must be practical indeed if it draw from him any reply except a great shout of laughter and a droll return. There is nothing like the habit of carrying arms to teach a people courtesy and good temper.

The "cocktails" went round with immense rapidity while we crossed Greytown bar, and stood to the southward; but we were gratified to observe that the man at the wheel, though frequently solicited, steadily refused to drink until the steamer should be brought to.

In about a couple of hours we reached the Colorado bar, and went in over it; twelve feet was the deepest water we could find. Rifles were now loaded in readiness for the alligators which lie in shoals along these rivers, and in a few moments the sharp crack of the American small-bores resounded from every part of the vessel. Presently attention was called to a " Dutchman," whose Swiss rifle refused to go off.

" Wall, now, R——," said a big Missourian, " may I be very blank if I didn't say that there gingerbread dug-out o' yours were no 'count. Blank! We've more of 'em down in Massoora than ever you see, and the children paint 'em green, and use 'em for popguns."

"Eh, R——," said another, very gravely; "won't that there gun o' yours go off? Ch—! How I have been admiring of it ever since I see the genteel poker it made when Mrs. R—— was a-stirring the kitchen fire a day 'gone. 'They're wonderful keen things,' she says to me, 'air Dutch guns! When they've got to know you, you may be just as cruel to 'em as you please, and they're that good-hearted they won't do yer any hurt.'"

The real fact was, Captain P—— had put a handful of lucifer matches down the barrel while it lay unloaded on deck.

The land at the mouth of the Colorado is even more swampy than in the neighbourhood of Greytown: we found the forest a foot deep in mud wherever it was tried. A German doctor on board told us there was an artficial hill somewhere near, on which were ruins, and the remains of a most wonderful pavement, the tiles of which were of slate and copper, fastened together horizontally, the slate uppermost. He said it was utterly impossible to chip the stone from the metal, so incredibly tenacious was the substance that united them. He had found numerous specimens, some of which were in the museum of Paris, some in that of Vienna, and some in New York. The fact is exceedingly curious, if true; but his notion of the locality of this hill was too vague to encourage us to penetrate the swamp, even with such wonders in view. There were a few Muscovy ducks on the shore, plenty of cranes and sandpipers, thousands of alligators, but no large game. Captain P—— shot a "congo," or howling monkey, which was secretly served up as guatuse, or jungle rabbit. When all had eaten heartily—for (I speak with the fear of all created old women before my eyes) few animals are more delicious than a young monkey—a long black paw, grasping a lighted candle, was handed round with the cigars. The horrid suspicion caused some pallor among the party, and one or two retired precipitately. Mr. Jebb and I were not at our first meal of monkey-flesh, and the joke missed fire.

We remained in the Colorado three days, surveying and cutting wood. Certainly in the course of a wandering life I never passed three days in such a strange scene. The drinking was carried to a pitch only equalled by the swearing, and both were varied and ingenious beyond English dreams. Gambling never ceased in the twenty-four hours. We might almost fill a volume with the drolleries seen and heard among our singular hosts. One wretched old gentleman, lying asleep on deck, was sewn up completely with strong twine. His coat was sewn to his shirt and jersey, his trousers to his coat, his socks to his trousers, and even his hat to his collar. When he awoke and rolled over, crack!—his whole apparel ripped up. Another victim, incautiously taking off his upper clothes to wash, found them put up as stakes, played for, and won, when he wished to dress again. Two members of the party got into their own pockets every penny there was on board, and another displayed eight penknives of his winning. The same poor fellow who lost his clothes had his boots drawn off while asleep. They were put on the table, won, and lost in three minutes, and all the complaints of the "Dutch" owner, on awakening, were received with shouts of laughter.

He was confined to the vessel in his stockings for the rest of the voyage, having the additional mortification of seeing the winner stroll about the deck with his handsome buff boots on, and of listening to critical comments on the make of the articles and estimate of their value. But everything was returned to its former owner on arrival at Greytown; even the money, which had been won fairly enough. One gentleman gave back more than fifty dollars.

I hope no one will think this description of our odd companion, tedious. To Nicaraguans, and in Nicaragua, their manners and habits are interesting in the highest degree. Such men as these were the fifty-five heroes who stood shoulder to shoulder in the plain of Rivas, and held their ground against odds of thirty to one. Such men as these were the four hundred who in Guadaloupe church lived for nineteen days upon the bodies of their comrades, rather than yield to the liberal terms offered by the thousands of their besiegers; and among us was a survivor of that wild band. Such men as these were the hundred and seventy-five who carried Granada in a night attack, routing three thousand troops, and storming three successive barricades. But, on the other hand, it was men like these who yielded to a mad panic at Santa Rosa, and fled before half their number of Costa Ricans. Before the castle of San Juan they fled again, and on the Serebpiqui. The list of their incomprehensible defeats is almost as long as that of their heroic victories. The turbulence and thoughtlessness of his army ruined Walker's scheme, as his knowledge of their reckless bravery had alone enabled him to conceive it.

In returning by the San Juan branch, we stayed from time to time to take in wood piled up on the river bank, and the removal of the logs was not performed without some danger. Snakes, and centipedes, and scorpions abounded; and while the men worked, we stood by with ready guns to greet them as they wriggled, half asleep, from under the overthrown faggots. Ah! the lovely scenes we can call to mind in those little clearings!—how at evening the sunbeams glinted among the crush of foliage!—how cool and quiet the steamer looked in the blue forest shadow! A rainbow light lay on the river, a red gleam upon the dead leaves at our feet, a glitter and glow upon the topmost branches of the tall trees. A ceaseless crash of overthrown logs, the short sharp cries of the Spaniards, the distant crack of a rifle deadened by the dense forest, the hum of a big beetle, and the gurgle of the river—these were the pleasant sounds that filled the drowsy hours. Then, suddenly, a shout and a scuffle. Amidst cries of "Tuboba! tuboba! Señor!" we hurry to the spot, and there, in a scene of wild confusion, we make our first acquaintance with that great snake, the terror of Central America, the beautiful black and brown "tuboba." *He* is not likely to wriggle away or try to hide himself. Knowing his deadly power, he stands steadily before us; his glassy eye looks straight in front; he does not deign to glance aside, though our every movement is marked. The long coils of his body, so soft and satiny, are quivering to the spring. His throat swells with rage and venom, and his head begins to sway with an almost imperceptible motion. For a moment we admire the graceful curve of that raised neck—and then the poor tuboba lies struggling upon the ground, with a bullet through his skull.

Once, too, we disturbed a pair of dull, stupid-looking lizards, at sight of which the workmen fled in dismay. They declared them to be so poisonous, that a mere touch with a booted foot would cause a horrible death.* I cut them to pieces with my knife.

But the insects and the creeping things we unhoused, how odd they were. Great spiders with basilisk eyes, which darted about in a strange zig-zag course; hairy beetles and flat cockroaches, which took to their wings and flew; flat soppy insects, of hideously uncertain shape, which rolled about under foot; shiny black crickets, with long inquisitive horns, which leaped up into the air, and struck us in the face.

* From Dr. Flint of Granada we received an account of a reptile most virulently poisonous. The first case in which it was brought under his notice was that of a man found dead one morning, with the complete impress of a lizard's body burnt into his back. A further search showed the body of the reptile, also dead; probably smothered by the weight of the man lying on it. The second case was that of a healthy young woman, who put her foot—hardened, by long habit of walking barefoot, into the consistency of leather, —upon one of these reptiles in the woods. Though Dr. Flint used every remedy he could devise, she finally died in great agony. This lizard seems to be almost transparent, small, and slow in its movements. A very slight pressure will crush it; a whitish liquid exudes from the body. Apparently those we found on the San Juan were not of this species.

But there were others also. Living jewels flashed about the displaced wood; lovely little frogs, that seemed made of scarlet sealing-wax, scrambled about our feet, and looked up with eyes of emerald and topaz; big iguanas, with coats of shining green, scuffled over the grass, carrying their long tails high up above their backs; flies of sapphire, with ruby wings, hung quivering in the sunbeams that pierced the tangled foliage.

When the pale evening mists began to climb the steamer's sides, the last logs were thrown on board, and we rejoined our party. "Kind o' pretty it were, that clearin'. Made one's eyes feel good, ye know,—the timber, and the sundown, and all! Will yer jine us? This is genuine Bourbon!"

CHAPTER II.

Californian Transit Company—The " Old Transit "—Captain Pim's scheme—The Governor of Greytown—Story of a Rio Frio expedition—Kidnapping a British subject—The river San Juan—Story of Mr. S——His domestic arrangements—Castillo Viejo—Rapids—San Carlos—Condition of the people—Mouth of the Frio river—Lake of Nicaragua—Ometepec—Zapatero—Indian reservations — Filibusters — Granada — Houses and customs—Hotel—Presidio—Churches—Siege and assault of the filibusters—Revolutions—Amusements—Scorpions—Hammock living.

GREYTOWN is the Atlantic terminus of the Californian Transit Company, an enterprise of which we in England know less than might be wished.* It is essentially an American speculation, and is specially favoured by the government of the United States; to the extent, as is whispered, of support from the public purse in its declining fortunes. The first company that opened this route, in 1852, is generally called the Vanderbilt;

* The apathy with which transit projects are received in England is very curious, and not a little suggestive to those who have seen the excitement with which any new scheme for crossing the continent is greeted in the States.

VOL. I.   D

but an unfortunate quarrel with the townspeople of San Juan speedily brought this earliest effort to disaster. The warehouses and offices of the Company were built upon a sandspit called Punt' Arenas, which lies opposite to the town. The mid-stream is shallow, but a deep channel follows either bank. When the quarrel became bitter, each party set to work "improving" its own channel, driving in piles, and making dams, with the object of choking its enemy's water. *Both* parties succeeded in this aim, and more injury was done to the river in two years than Nature unaided would probably have wrought in ten. But at length the hostility became murderous, and the Vanderbilt Company—by shameless intrigue which would, I really think, have been impossible in any European government—caused the bombardment of Greytown by U.S.S. "Cyane," Captain Hollins, whose name should surely be handed down to posterity. On the 13th July, 1854, the little town, which had just begun to flourish, was burnt to the ground. The following letter, which cannot be too widely circulated in England, speaks for itself:—

"*Office of the Nicaraguan Line,*
"*New York, June 16, 1854.*

"Captain Hollins, commanding the corvette, "Cyane," leaves on Monday. You will see by his instructions, which I have written on the margin, that it is intended his authority *should not be so exercised as to show any mercy to the town or people.*

"If the scoundrels are soundly punished, we can take possession, and build it up as a business place, put in our own officers, transfer the jurisdiction, and *you know the rest.*

"It is of the last importance that the people of the town should be taught to fear us. Punishment will teach them. After which you must agree with them as to the organisation of a new government, and the officers of it. Everything now depends on you and Hollins. The latter is all right. He fully understands the outrage, and will not hesitate in enforcing reparation.

"I hope to hear from you that all has been properly executed.

"I am, &c.,

"J. L. WHITE.

"*To* Mr. J. W. FABENS,
"*Cons. Agent of the U. S. at Greytown.*"

And "properly executed" Greytown was accordingly. There is *something* of the old Roman about the Yankee Republic.

But retribution soon followed. Up to 1855 the Transit, flourished exceedingly, and the Company ran a hard race with the Panama Railway ; but in that year the filibusters came down on Nicaragua. General Walker was not a man to bear injustice or to heed bullying from his own countrymen more than from others ; and he promptly served the Vanderbilt Company with a notice to pay the $400,000 which had been long due to Nicaragua.* Their refusal was followed by the seizure of the steamers on river and lake ; but the Vanderbilt sent out a daring soldier of fortune named Spencer, who recaptured the vessels one by one, and thereby ruined the filibusters. But the Company never recovered this blow.

After its financial decease there was peace on the San Juan for some years, and the needle-ducks and the bull-frogs and the spurwings

* For details of the successive Transit Companies, their charters and operations, I must refer the reader to that valuable book, " The Gate of the Pacific," by Captain Bedford Pim, whose own scheme of a Transatlantic railway will be found there.

had it all their own way on land and river. But in 1862 some merchants of New York, evil-starred, took up the enterprise, and ever since they have been playing ducks and drakes on the San Juan with twenty-dollar pieces. After a certain number of leaps and falls, the coin invariably sinks to the bottom of the river, where in all probability it will ever remain.

The route from New York is by sea as far as this town; then by the river San Juan and the Lake of Nicaragua to Virgin Bay; thence twelve miles by land to San Juan del Sur; and thence to San Francisco by the Pacific. The cause of financial failure to the Company lies—firstly, in the excessive lowness of the fare ($35 only); secondly, bad management in "connection," the ocean steamers frequently failing to meet the passengers at their arrival on the coast; in which case the whole expense of maintaining the passengers falls upon the Company. And, most hopeless of all, the gradual silting-up of the San Juan River, and consequent growth of the bar. Twenty years ago the harbour of Greytown is described by travellers as "magnificent," capable of containing ships of any tonnage; but when we arrived there was barely eight feet of water at the mouth, and during our stay the port became absolutely locked: a channel was hastily cut to let off the rising water. In fact, it is evident that Greytown is doomed. By damming up the Colorado arm of the San Juan Delta, it might indeed be possible to pour such an impetuous flood into the northern branch as to sweep out all obstruction, and partially, at least, to recreate a port; but independently of the danger of the work in a country so low and swampy, such a piece of engineering is quite beyond the means of the present Company, hampered by debt and ruined in credit as it is. At this moment, after a vain attempt to establish a terminus at the mouth of the Colorado, the Company is endeavouring to close the Toro, a smaller branch of the Delta, and to turn its waters into the San Juan. Such an attempt was made unsuccessfully some years ago. Having lately, with the aid of the United States government, it is whispered, effected a loan of $3,000,000, the Company may probably succeed in their object, but the relief would scarcely be for months. In descending from

Costa Rica by the Serebpiqui, we positively walked nearly half the distance from Machuca Rapids in the bed of the river, as there was not water enough to float our canoe. And where all was so shallow that the simple precaution of turning up our trousers kept us dry, the shallowest part appeared to be *above* the Toro fork.

It seems to be well authenticated that long after the conquest, sea-going vessels of the period could and did sail direct from Europe up the San Juan to Granada. Thomas Gage, the English traveller, says so distinctly of the year 1665, and also that ships for ocean service were built on the lake. At present the rapids of Machuca and Toro would effectually bar the passage of any vessel drawing over four feet of water, and under the old fort there is scarcely six inches of depth. It is asserted that the rapids of the San Juan were wilfully formed by Spain, to keep out the buccaneers. Certainly they are little heard of till modern times.* Even in 1780 they do not seem to have been insurmountable, when the English sailed up to the lake. The river also was very deep at that time, for Nelson

* *Vide* Chapter V.

ascended as far as Mico Island in his corvette, the "Henchenbrok," a feat quite impossible for very many years past. In fact, the inhabitants of Greytown, whose existence is bound up in Transit schemes, mournfully admit that the town is "played out." No other harbour is available. Monkey Point has long been ceded to Captain Bedford Pim, as the Atlantic terminus of his projected railroad, and no port exists to the southward. The Transit Company is, I believe, doomed; and it is scandalously whispered that they hold on still only in the hope that they may be bought out by the necessities of some railroad or canal scheme.

On our return to Greytown we at once engaged passage on the freight boat starting in two days for Granada. It therefore became necessary to call on the Governor about passports; for, though I was furnished, Mr. Jebb had not taken such precaution in London. We found at Government House a burly personage who was quite unable to pronounce a word of English, though nine-tenths of the people of Greytown are Americans, or negroes speaking our tongue. The report given to us of government energy was quite funny. In case of a row among the Transit passengers,—and a voyage seldom passes without one,—the representative of order waits patiently until it is fought out. When some wretch is shot or bowied, and the guilty party safe held in the hands of the bystanders, he strolls to the spot with some majesty, and claims the malefactor in the name of the law. After carefully noting down the circumstances of the affair—what a valuable collection of fighting stories must lie in the archives of Greytown!—the accused is put to work in the garden of Government House, and otherwise made useful until the next steamer shall arrive. He is then, provided the government ground has been properly dug and planted with garlic, dispatched to New York at his own expense.

But the scandal of Greytown, though more amusing than most others, is peculiarly liable to mislead.

In the course of a very cordial conversation, the Governor told us the tale of an expedition organized by the Commandante of San Carlos in 1849, to explore the Rio Frio. We subsequently heard many versions of this disastrous affair, which has caused much of the terror felt for the Guatusos; but a man occupying a position so important as the government of Greytown ought certainly to be well informed upon the subject, and I repeat the story briefly as he told it us.

I have already stated that the Rio Frio falls into the lake of Nicaragua about three hundred yards from the spot at which the San Juan flows out of it, and is consequently almost opposite to the fort of San Carlos. The Commandante of this post, dwelling within sight of the mysterious stream, and wearied, we may suppose, of the dreary idleness to which he was condemned in a little ruinous village, determined to investigate the Guatuso marvel, at the head of a force too strong for resistance. It should be observed that Nicaragua and Costa Rica are at variance in regard to their frontier line; and loud the Guatusos would laugh if they could hear the bold claims laid by each republic to a territory which neither of them dare approach. At the time of the San Carlos expedition Nicaragua was much more powerful than at present, and she treated little Costa Rica with calm contempt.

Accordingly the Commandante fitted out a large boat with everything necessary for his frugal soldiery, and embarked with fifty picked men.*

On the fifth day many footsteps of Indians were noted on the river bank, together with rude huts, plantain patches, and other signs of cultivation. Each night the party landed, and camped ashore. On the sixth morning the footprints around their bivouac were so numerous, and showed such daring in approach, as to cause the Commandante some uneasiness. The same thing happened on the seventh morning, but the enemy's force had again increased. At noon on this disastrous day the party halted to rest; for the stream had dwindled to a volume so small as scarcely to admit the boats, and the labour was severe. On landing, the soldiers did not even retain their side-arms; guns, bayonets, and machetes were left in a light canoe. As they lay round in the shade, smoking and cooking, they were suddenly overwhelmed by a very rain of

---

* It would appear that the army of Nicaragua was much more numerous in those days: at present the whole force at San Carlos is not fifty soldiers.

arrows, which killed numbers on the spot, and wounded nearly all the others. A rush was made to the canoe containing arms, and it was overturned in the tumult. The shower of arrows still continued, and men fell thickly. Losing all presence of mind, the survivors broke, and fled singly into the woods. The Commandante, wounded in sixteen places, managed to conceal himself till nightfall, when he crept down to the river bank; and, by following the stream, succeeded in reaching San Carlos after fearful hardships. Two more of the party subsequently turned up, but one of them died immediately on arrival. So ended the most important attempt to explore the Rio Frio that has been made in modern times.

I should observe, however, that, by other accounts, nearly half the expedition made its way back to the fort. In a country like Nicaragua it is impossible to ascertain the truth of any story one year after date; but if there be twenty, or even ten or five survivors of this disaster still alive, it seems odd they should never have communicated with us, when the report of our intended exploration was so widely spread.

Mr. Squier also, who reached San Carlos, as he says himself, only " some months " after the affair, asserts that the Commandante *alone* returned ; and the German traveller Frœbel, four years afterwards, makes the same statement. No light whatever was thrown upon the habits of the Guatusos or the nature of their country by this expedition : the Commandante never wandered from his boats, and the jungle was very dense. Not even in the heat of the massacre did a single Indian warrior show himself, and this fact has added not a little to the superstition with which these fierce savages are regarded.

After telling us this story, the worthy Governor put his house at our disposal with much fervour, but we preferred the hotel. On returning thither, we found the sister of our little Jamaica boy, Sammy. Her errand was soon explained : she had changed her mind about letting the boy follow our fortunes. We pointed out that it was a little late to alter the arrangement, as he had already presented an order upon our agent for various garments, of which he was much in need ; but that if she were indeed his lawful guardian, we would not oppose her authority. With this she went away. Presently appeared Sammy himself, who declared that his sister was " no 'count," and that he meant to go with us in spite of every one. We applauded these sentiments, and offered him such encouragement as we could devise without infringing the Church Catechism,—to wit, that paragraph about pastors and masters, and those set in authority.

On the day of departure our luggage was put into a big boat and sent to the steamer, while we walked through the brushwood to the Company's wharf. In a few moments we were joined by Sammy, very pale, but big with a great resolve. Before he had time to explain himself, however, he gave a start and a bound, and instantaneously disappeared among the clumps of sand-apple and tangle. Here he rapidly formed himself in light skirmishing order, while his terror, in a yellow dress and crimson hat, hurried past us with scowling brows. Evidently there was fun at hand. We pressed forward. From time to time a glimpse was caught of our devoted boy darting from bush to bush in agonized bounds; but he displayed so much genius in concealing himself, that we were always in doubt as to his position. But on observing the movements of the enemy, we marked a dreadful decision about them, and a horrid craft, which made us sigh for Sammy. Poor little victim! In pitiful fancy we could see him dragged back through those bushes, attached to the yellow dress, and gazing in agony upon the crimson *chapeau*, while the tears ran down his innocent cheeks. Were they innocent, his cheeks? I don't know. He was very sharp; but I don't think he had committed murder, and I am tolerably sure he had never been treasurer to a savings' bank, so at Greytown he would be called innocent. We noted that the enemy was making direct for the wharf, while Sammy, in his wild panic and overpowering anxiety to avoid being seen, was bounding along at something like right angles to his proper course, and in a few moments must have taken his final leap into the Atlantic, where he would have been hidden from mortal view for evermore. Therefore, in the confidence that he would guide himself by our movements, we pushed on, and again passed the enemy. A great change had come over her appearance. Whereas at the first encounter it was difficult to mark the line at which the yellow dress was gathered around her throat, so now was it impossible to distinguish crimson hat from crimson visage. Family affection is a sacred feeling, honoured in every virtuous mind : to exercise the authority of a parent without his cares is sweet to the feminine spirit, and much affected by elder sisters; but before I would have made myself as hot as did that devoted woman, I would have seen all my little Jamaica brothers back in the land of their nativity. With what haste had she rushed forth, clad in the simple garment of the domestic circle ! What a touching sacrifice of vanity, thus unadorned to show herself on the fashionable wharf!

Sammy now gave a leap into the midst of a guava bush and disappeared, leaving us in doubt whether he had passed ahead, or whether he lay deep down under the grey waves of the ocean. We hurried on, and the enemy hurried after. We came in sight of the steamer; no Sammy !

The vessel was lying, with fires up, about three feet from the narrow jetty, and a plank was laid down for passengers. At the end of this plank did the enemy take up her red and yellow position, scowling indiscriminately at every one about the wharf. In another moment Sammy made his appearance, still aimlessly skirmishing from bush to bush, though in full view of fifty people who had run down to see the fun. Encouraged by the cheering cries which greeted him, and stimulated by the sight of his goal, he made a rush upon the wharf, dodged the enemy round a big anchor, escaped her clutch by a miracle, and then, in a great bound of desperation, leaped on board. "Hi, Sammy!" "Who-oop, Sammy!" "'Think o' Jerusalem and the land o' promise—whoop!" "Go slow, go slow, old lady! Wet yer claws and think o' cotton!" "Whoop, koo-oo!" How we all laughed! Such a chase there was among the scattered cargo— then by the wood pile—then a rush up the steps to the hurricane deck—the agonised face of Sammy—the grim wrath of his avenging sister —Heaven grant us all such hearty fun from time to time until we die!

At length the enemy was disheartened, out of breath, and mad with "chaff." After a moment's pause she strode off towards the Governor's house, muttering fierce threats to have her brother "if there was law in Greytown!" Mean time the Transit people—who, with the ready good-nature in which we never knew one of their officers to fail, took the greatest interest in the matter—worked with enthusiasm to get the steamer off, and at length, just as a boat put from the town, we were fairly away. Steam was up in a moment and we went full speed, but the pursuers gained on us, having but to pull straight to intercept our course. Through our glasses could be made out a white man sitting in the stern and gesticulating wildly, but poor Sammy, who was with us on the hurricane deck, could not hold the glass steady enough to identify him. Certainly no Transit steamer since the days of Walker had crossed the harbour at such a pace as did ours, but still the canoe was gaining. Suddenly there is a shout of triumph; she has struck on a covered sand-bar and half filled. We pass by with bitter mockery before the obstacle is rounded. Sammy is carried off to unknown dangers, and we enjoy the glorious reputation of kidnappers.

The San Juan river runs through a marshy

plain as devoid of interest as of beauty. There
are certain points of difference between the
Eastern and Western Tropics which cannot fail
to strike any traveller. Firstly, in the size of
the timber. I know there are immense trees in
America, larger perhaps than any Asiatic species;
but I fearlessly assert that the average of forest
timber on the former continent is smaller and
lower by a third than that of the latter. The
great tree of Nagarote, one of the shows of
Nicaragua, and a boast for miles, would be considered a very ordinary object beside a fairly-
grown "tapong" of Borneo or banian of Hin-
dostan. Secondly, in the quantity and richness
of the flowers; there America is unrivalled.
Every bit of waste ground, every open spot in
the forest is overrun with brilliant blossom;
even the sea-sand is hidden by flowering shrubs
and tangles of pink convolvulus. The densest
thicket, to which the sun can never creep, will
boast some hardy flower, and the tree tops are
ablaze with crimson and gold. But that majesty
of the Eastern jungle, which strikes the least im-
pressible traveller with a feeling of awe, is lost
among the smaller trees and brighter colours of

the Western forest. There is no silence, no solemnity; the great black "congos" howl dismally all the day through; parrots scream, jays twitter, paroquets chirp overhead. The woods of America are crammed with beasts and birds, and every one of them makes a noise.

Among our fellow-passengers was a filibuster from Texas: he was a tall, sallow man, perfectly good-tempered, most obliging, overflowing with the oddest humour, yet celebrated as one of the readiest fellows with the pistol to be found among the remnants of Walker's army. He it was who accompanied Captain P—— to a fandango in Greytown, where the latter was nearly cut in two by a machete blow from behind. Of all the awful wounds I ever saw that is the most terrible, and how it could possibly be survived I cannot conceive. On feeling the blow, P—— called upon S—— and two other foreigners in the room, and then, holding his flesh up round his waist, he snatched up a stool in his right hand, and, as he says, "went in." S—— used no weapon at all—probably because he had none with him—but joined his old commander with his fists, and what is termed generally "wild-cat work" in Texas. How many were gouged or hugged, how many had limbs broken, nobody knows; but in five minutes seventy natives were thrown out of the room, and not ten went by the door. As the last of them fled howling up the street, or was carried away by his companions, P—— fell fainting on the floor, and S—— was detained in attending to him while help was coming. In the mean time the coward who struck the blow had fled in a canoe, and never since has he ventured to return to his wife and family in Greytown. In process of time P—— recovered, and claimed compensation, to which he was somehow entitled; but the American consul declined to advocate his case, because both he and S—— "had expressed sympathy with the Southern rebels!"*

* To illustrate the incredible recklessness of life so characteristic of the filibuster class, I may mention an anecdote of this gentleman, for which we can vouch. Lying in his hammock on the hurricane deck, S—— was much pestered by the invitations of a Californian friend to go to the bar; invitations he was too lazy to accept. The Californian became very angry, and, drawing his revolver, threatened to shoot unless his filibuster friend would come. This was no idle threat, as all knew, but S—— composedly observed—"Shoot away! You're too tight to hit a haystack if the wind were high." The Californian fired two shots quick as thought, and not till then did S—— slowly cock his revolver, drawling, "That's enough, I guess. If you pull again, *I'*ll shoot!"

Mr., or Captain, S——, had a small plantation by Machuca rapids. On landing there, in a pouring rain, to take in wood, we were presented to his wife, a pretty little Creole, who could not speak a word of English. As S—— could not get beyond the oaths in Spanish, their household was singularly peaceful. After surveying this couple for some time, we saw clearly the secret of domestic happiness, and resolved that in marrying we would seek the same conditions. I think it probable that Adam and Eve spoke different languages in Paradise.

After two days' journey over the muddy San Juan, during which the rain never ceased for two hours at a time, we reached Castillo Viejo, the fort celebrated in Nicaragua as having been besieged but *not captured* by the great Nelson. European history, however, seems to disagree with the native story upon this latter point, and thinks that the present ruin of the fortification is principally to be attributed to the dismantling it then underwent at the hands of English sailors. Possibly European history is wrong, but it seems more probable that the error should lie with Nicaragua. At this place is the Custom House, but the officials were very polite, as they always are, and did not examine our baggage. Here we changed steamers.

On the following morning an individual, who looked just like Robinson Crusoe, and proved to be equally amiable and interesting, was introduced to us by the captain. In spite of his long hair, ragged beard, and generally wild appearance, we found him to be a man wonderfully educated for the country : he spoke English very well, fair French, and Spanish much superior to the usual patois. The poor fellow's history was one only too common here. He had been wealthy, and was allied with all the best families of Nicaragua, the Chamorros, the Lacayos, and the rest; but the filibuster war had destroyed his house, ruined his plantations, killed or driven off all his cattle herds, and at its close he found himself, with many of his family, absolutely penniless. Fortunately he was unmarried, and, as he told us, managed to rub along, living from day to day, like nine-tenths of the people. He introduced us to a lady, his cousin, also ruined by the civil wars. She was living with a son and daughter in a cane-built hut, in no way distinguishable from those of the other inhabitants, but her manners were worthy of the old Spanish blood she boasted. Certainly we never saw better " style," though her residence was not fit for a well-bred dog. This lady, who had never travelled out of Nicaragua, asked us in perfect seriousness what we thought of her " town," and whether people were so comfortable in England. Her " town " consisted of thirty pigsties, and a hundred dirty natives, half-naked. Of course we thought she was making a small joke, and were just about to reply in kind, when the cousin, who knew something of the world, warned us in English that the question was quite serious, and that we should give deep offence if we did not make a complimentary reply. We told him to tell the necessary fibs himself: being a Roman Catholic, he could get indulgence for them.

By means of this obliging acquaintance we were enabled to visit the castle, which few Europeans have entered in peaceful fashion. A quaint, picturesque old fortress it is: strength there is positively none, since the most modern cannon we could find bore the date of seventeen hundred and something;* but the people look upon it with immense superstition, and the Commandante, who sat in his shirt-sleeves affably smoking among the garrison, is an important personage in Nicaragua. While we were at breakfast ashore—a breakfast consisting of cakes made of *fried hogs' blood*, pork fat mixed with chillies and boiled in an envelope of dough, half-ripe plantains, boiled, and dirty chocolate, intensely bitter and greasy—the steamer was forcing its way up the rapids with the safety valve screwed down and a bucket-full of old iron hung on to the lever. These rapids of Castillo Viejo are the most dangerous on the river: the yellow water leaps and swirls in a manner really terrific, and no clear space occurs in the length and breadth of the descent. Indeed, it should rather be called a long cataract than a rapid; the fall is about six feet in two hundred yards, and the shallow bottom is of broken rock. In an accident there is no possibility of saving life, though the overturned canoe be close to the bank. Over and over the body is rolled, rocks tear it limb

---

* Captain Bedford Pim says there are two dismounted guns taken from the filibusters on the works, but we did not see them.

from limb, back eddies carry it into deep recesses and whirl it for minutes beneath the surface; the last throb of the water vomits it forth a mass of shapeless flesh.

Wonderful to relate, though accidents of divers sorts have sunk no less than twenty-six steamers in the river and lake, no mishap has ever occurred in the ascent of these rapids. With a safety-valve screwed down, and a bucket of lead, or two if necessary, hanging to the lever, a steamer* is driven up this terrific incline, now giving ground, now mounting, now held stationary by the vast force of water, just as a living thing would be in the same attempt. In our case the ascent was made in half an hour; and the vessel lay to round the point, to be loaded with the heavy cargo discharged at the foot of the rapids, and sent across the promontory by a tramway. Then we rejoined her and passed on to San Carlos.

It is believed that these rapids were designedly made the almost impassable obstruction they now are by the casting of big rocks into the channel.

* The passengers are discharged at either end of the rapid, walk across the promontory, and a fresh steamer takes them up or down. We went on in the same vessel.

Dread of English buccaneers induced this suicidal measure on the part of the Spaniards. The most notable event in the history of Castillo Viejo, besides its capture by Nelson, is the siege of the Leonese party therein by Fruto Chamorro, at the head of the Grenadinos. On the taking of the place every soul in it was put to death in cold blood. Verily, barbarism works its own reward. During the filibuster war, Castillo Viejo was captured by Walker, and recaptured by the Costa Ricans, under Mr. Spencer and Colonel Cauty. By the latter it was defended during the second siege of the filibusters under Colonel Titus. Colonel Cauty is an Englishman.

The cultivation on the San Juan is a joke. Here and there lies a plantain patch, surrounding a wood-pile or a tumble-down shed, at which horrible spirits are sold to the thirsty Transit passengers, or to naked bongo men. But one clearing alone on the river is entitled to the name of plantation. This belongs to a Mr. Wolfe, a Prussian naval officer, who has resided in Nicaragua for twenty years. He says the soil is everything that could be wished, the climate most healthy, and the country in every respect suited to extensive cultivation. Difficulty of obtaining labour is the bar to all success. Mr. Wolfe cultivates coffee and cacao. But certainly, as a family residence, the San Juan does not appear to fill all requisites : the only amusement for the ladies of a household is to watch the alligators, to keep an eye on the " tubobas," and to root out the scorpions. Passing bongos, or row barges, might afford some little entertainment, were it not that the stark nakedness of the crew makes observation indelicate, while their inveterate thievishness discourages any acquaintance. Dozens of these clumsy vessels we met on our way up, many of them carrying female passengers ; but, delicacy or no delicacy, the bongo men did not wear a stitch of clothing, not even when stopping for a moment at the houses. Only at the end of their voyage, Granada, or at its beginning, Greytown, do they practise the merest sign of decency.

At eight o'clock on the third evening we reached San Carlos, and announced our approach with the deepest roar our steam-pipe was capable of uttering. After several repetitions of a thunder audible for miles around, the garrison of San Carlos seemed all at once to catch the sound, and sallied forth with flaming torches, a response which every vessel must await before approaching this terrible fortress. The lake steamer was already awaiting us, and we went on board.

Next morning we put off in a canoe, and paddled to shore. Such a wretched, tumble-down hamlet it was. The streets were paved with rough stones, and traces of a built wharf were still observable, but the huts were dingy and ruinous. In former times a town of some importance stood at this point, and the pavement still remaining gives token of its advancement; but it was sacked by buccaneers, battered by Nelson, burnt in civil wars, and blown up by filibusters, until its only remains are a few ruinous blocks of masonry overgrown with creepers, and the pebbly pavement aforesaid. We strolled up the hilly street, and over a rocky bit of grass land, towards a massive archway which still stood erect, bearing upon its shoulders a tangled thicket of trees and shrubs. In the deep groove, through which the portcullis used to slide, was now a mud-built nest of stinging flies; in and out between the ponderous stones wound endless lines of ants; bats hung like a fringe in the deep cool shadow of the roof. Upon the other side were heavy walls, starred over with blue convolvulus, and draped with long festoons of creepers: gemlike butterflies, and lizards almost as brilliant, sunned themselves on the ruined steps. Beyond, a mighty tower lay prostrate, its shapeless fragments buried in a network of shrubs and twining "vines." As these grand ruins are to the dirty sheds of the modern town, so is Spain even now, in her decay and misery, to the wretched republics which cast off her yoke. Heaven forbid I should justify the Spanish system of colonial government; but is it possible that under any, even the worst, of European rules, these four states, Guatemala, San Salvador, Nicaragua, and Honduras, could have reached such a point of mean and despicable misery as that to which they have brought themselves in forty years of independence? The virtues of civilized man have deserted these lovely countries; and those common among savages, hospitality, subordination to their chiefs, family affection, have not yet arisen; nor can that manliness, the stock from which they should grow, as yet be noticed. On the other hand, neither reading nor hard experience have made us acquainted with a single bad quality from which the mass of these people are exempt. Lying, and cowardice, and dishonesty are the qualities which every foreigner attributes to the whole upper class. Every member of that class, in private conversation, will tell you that the race is utterly perverse and rotten,—of course, with an understood exception in favour of himself. I can safely say that out of hundreds of influential men with whom we have spoken, there were not ten who did not *spontaneously* bewail the degradation of their race, and anxiously discuss the chance of foreign intervention. No matter from whence it comes, United States, France, England, or even Italy— anywhere except Spain—a rule of white men is eagerly desired by every influential person in the country. For it should be remembered that the population of Nicaragua is not white. Two-fifths are Indians of unmixed blood, two-fifths mestizos, or Indian half-breeds, and the remaining fifth negro, or mulatto, or Sambo. Possibly there may be ten families in the whole country whose genealogical tree, if it possessed one, could show an ancestry of European blood unmixed; but of those we saw, judging from their outward appearance only, which is the lightest test of all, one stock alone, the Chamorro, seemed to us to present sufficient signs of purity.

The mixture of negro blood is very large in some districts, and the black race in general is not regarded with any particular contempt. Indeed, it is difficult to see on what grounds the Nicaraguan should despise the negro; but that is no reason, as we all know. On the other hand, the "Jamaica Creole" will look upon the "Greaser" with the same ineffable pity he feels for the true "nigger"—"Dam black head'n from Sarah Leon." In point of work they are about equal, or, if anything, the negro is more industrious. He keeps himself quiet usually, and in general has a small sum of dollars hidden away in a handkerchief out of reach of ants. In fact, wherever the negro finds himself in a minority, he behaves as a worthy and industrious member of society—witness Canada, the Northern States, the East Indies; but if, by force of any circumstances, he become the more numerous section of the community, instantly his bad instincts get the upper hand, and the hopeless negro barbarism, which has been since the world began and ever will remain, breaks out after a century's torpor. He is again the childish, sensual savage his father was. What then is to be done with him in Jamaica, in Secessia, and elsewhere, the countries in which he forms such an immense portion of the population? A question delightfully easy to—ask! We have brought him from that land so pestilential to white men— in which Providence or Natural Selection placed him, that he might play his fantastic tricks by himself—and for certain purposes have transferred him to the Eden-like isles where he now riots in drink, and debauchery, and idolatry, and madness, and murder, amidst the plaudits of foolish clergymen at Exeter Hall. To enslave him again is out of the question. Every negro in the islands would fight like a wild cat in defence of his idleness, and no one among us dreams of that universal massacre which, sooner or later, will settle the question in the States. I would recommend a strong measure, but that our backs have grown so weak with age, and with that philanthropy which is hysteria, that we have no longer nerve for anything strong except religion. In France and in America they are young yet. There the old women stay at home and do their appointed work, while the chiefs sit round the council fire, and the young men go out to fight. When the victory is gained, and the warriors return, the old women proudly count the head trophies, and hang them up in the pangaran house, and sing of the valour of their tribe. What would be said to them if they held their own councils upon the conduct of the war, and passed the chiefs in review, and deafened the house with their squeaking and screaming? Surely a great shout of laughter from the *men* who did the work would silence these aged dames, who have no longer the strength, and never had the courage, to go forth into the deadly jungle, to fight for the honour of the tribe and the safety of the little ones. Much have we to learn from the French—more, I sometimes think, than we have to teach. We can convert them from the detestable errors of Popery,—that is, of course, if they care about being converted. We can put them up to a few things in steam and machinery,—not so very many now, they tell us. We can introduce roast beef more generally,—though I am glad to observe that joints are regularly served now, *chez Bignon père*, and at the Café Riche. Verily, I see nothing more in which our lights can benefit the Parisians. On the other hand, what can they teach us? Firstly, they may return the compliment about those " detestable errors;" then again, in cooking; then, and then, and then—I decline to point out the other superiorities of the French nation. But could we not, on occasion, call up a *little* of their nerve, and imitate, at any distance, their manner of laughing down and disregarding the screams of their old women?

The population of San Carlos is about two hundred souls. The houses are built of bamboos and branches, wattled together, and covered with mud and cow-dung. At the door of each hut is a filthy table or rough board, on which stand a few bottles of fancy compounds, called ginevra, or aguardiente, or cognacé, but which might be indiscriminately labelled vitriol and cane juice. The interior of the hut is furnished with a hide bed, swarming with vermin, an oven of clay, a twine hammock, two odd cups of English crockery, a stone for grinding tortillas, and a big bunch of green plantains. Sometimes there is a second chamber, divided from the saloon by a partition of bamboos about six inches apart. The use of this cage-like apartment I know not; because, independently of the fact that modesty is a virtue little practised in Nicaragua, there is no privacy whatever about it, and the traveller is at liberty to enter there as anywhere else. The floor is composed of the primeval mud beaten hard by the bare feet of the inmates, and alive with fleas and "neguas." These latter pests are better known in England by their West Indian name, "jiggers," or "chigos." As every one knows, they bury themselves in the foot, and there lay eggs, making a horrible sore if left to themselves.

The inhabitants of San Carlos are not agreeable in any way. They are poor; that they cannot help if they won't work. They are also dirty, which, with the lake within ten yards of them, is the effect of their natural filthiness. We saw a letter the other day from Professor

Seemann, in which he stated, that in travelling three weeks with certain Nicaraguans of the upper class, not one of them washed his face or hands during that time; and we can assure Professor Seemann, that if he had travelled three months with some individuals we encountered, he would not have seen them wash three times. With which dirty truth we bid good-bye to San Carlos the dirty.*

It is not such an easy thing to paddle your own canoe, as those who execute the feat lyrically might suppose, and so Mr. D—— found when attempting to navigate himself to the steamer. He whirled round and round in a manner as funny to the bystanders as bewildering to himself, now going one way, now the other, alternately red with exertion and pale with dizziness, but never moving three feet from his axis, which travelled parallel to the shore. Great fun it was to the natives, one of whom we sent into the water to get him out. We ourselves returned in a canoe so ragged and holey

* It is only fair to remark that some of the Nicaraguans are scrupulously cleanly; but of course I speak of the mass of the population, which is filthy.

that the sharks must have watched our progress with immense interest.

In the afternoon we rowed to the mouth of the awful Frio river, which lies about three hundred yards to the westward of the San Juan. At this end of the lake tall sedges run far out into the shallow water, and the passage of the big alligators can be traced by the bend and rustle of their feathery crowns. Half rowing, half punting, we made our way through this dangerous obstruction, and were not a little glad to strike clear water again. The alligators rose and sank in their oily manner all round us, and several times we could almost have touched a flat, scaly tail, one flick of which would have broken up our little dingy. I have always felt a particular disgust in thinking it possible that my flesh should go towards the swelling and fattening of that hideous, ill-proportioned, puncheon-like mass of deformity called an alligator. I never placed an overdue value upon the material of which I chance to be composed: there would be no horror on the part of my disembodied spirit if that material went towards the rounding of a tiger's muscles, or the sleeking of a great boa; but to become part of an alligator, that shapeless, bloated, unformed monster,—the thought is sickening.

The mouth of the Rio Frio is about seventy yards broad. Commonplace enough it seemed, that reed-blocked entrance to the mysterious land. The banks were a swamp of sedge and marsh grass, from which sprang a few poverty-stricken trees and a scanty growth of shrubs. On a dreary, damp spit we landed, to pick up a macaw, but the coarse blades cut our clothes like knives, leeches swarmed about our feet, and stinging ants attacked every inch of exposed flesh. Pushing on over the dusky waters, we came to a line of trees something like mangrove, and then to a very garden of convolvulus. Nothing could be seen but broad green leaves and garlands of varied blossom, white, and flesh tint, and scarlet, and pink, and, loveliest of all, deep blue. Others there were fantastically streaked and mottled, and in the midst of the garden, which covered an acre, stood a bush one mass of golden blossom. Further on we entered heavier forest. Here and there a tall tree leant across the stream, trailing its long beards of moss in the sluggish current. Another was spangled over with the crimson and yellow flowers of lianas; and another was twisted into a spiral column by the strain and pressure of the climber. On every bough an iguana sat, warming his motley scales and serrated crest in the hot sun; while, with green and glistening eyes, he stealthily watched our movements. Flocks of parrots passed overhead in that fluttering flight so peculiar to their kind, every pair keeping faithfully by itself, and breathlessly sympathising in musical croak. Big fish-hawks hung motionless in the sky, asleep on quivering wings; rows of uncouth needle-ducks were perched on every rotting snag, stupidly stretching their long wings as if for instant flight. With a sudden swirl and splash the great head of an alligator shot up above the surface, casting high into the air a fish, which he caught as it fell with a clash like the shutting of monstrous shears; then sinking down again so gently, so swiftly, so noiselessly, that he seemed rather to melt into the water.

The Lake of Nicaragua has never been properly surveyed, and all statements of length and breadth are little more than guesses. Captain Bailly puts it down as one hundred miles long by forty to forty-five broad. Mr. Squier thinks it full one hundred and twenty miles long, and forty to forty-five broad. The greatest depth that Captain Bailly could find was forty fathoms, and he considers the average to be from eight to twenty. Mr. Squier takes a broad average of ten to forty fathoms. Captain Bedford Pim's estimate would seem to be much smaller than either of these. In general, the depth will be found to increase towards the north and east; the southern shore is swampy and shallow. Numerous islands stud the water. On the southern shore are the three volcanic mountains of Ometepec, Madera, and Zapatero; and nearer Granada is a group of lava reefs called the " corales," or the thousand isles.

The island of Ometepec contains also the extinct volcano of Madera, and its name, Ome-Tepec, in pure Aztec, signifies two peaks. The loftier of these twin mountains is generally admitted to be the highest point in Nicaragua; but estimates vary, from M. Scherzer's of four thousand one hundred feet, to M. Tavernier's of six thousand five hundred. Of late years the tendency of travellers has been to give a greater elevation to Ometepec and its rival Mombacho; and I think the height marked by Captain Gregory's aneroid, six thousand two hundred feet, is nearly correct. According to our observations, this would seem to be barely one hundred feet higher than Mombacho. The island is believed by Mr. Squier to have been inhabited by an Aztec colony called Niquirans, who seem to have settled upon the neighbouring mainland, and he gives a number of Mexican words recovered from the Ometepec Indians. Mr. Squier was very fortunate in overcoming the distrust which has prevented these people from confiding to others the remains of their language which may still exist. But the difficulty of explaining how a word signifying "two peaks" could possibly be applied to one peak only, which is as regular as a sugarloaf, has been pointed out by Mr. Squier's friend, Dr. Frœbel. Mexican names are found in every part of Central America, far removed from the Niquiran settlements; and I can assert that the present Indians know nothing of their meaning. Upon this most interesting question I shall speak on reaching Chontales.

Before the time of Walker, Ometepec was a "reservation" for the separate use of the aborigines; but that high-handed dictator did away with this privilege—an injustice which bitterly exasperated the Indian population. On the overthrow of the filibusters, the national government retained this unjust annexation in spite of all remonstrance; and colonists of white or mixed blood now settle upon the island without the old permits from the Indian authorities. It was several times remarked to us that fears were to be entertained of serious difficulties to arise from this prolonged illegality. It is thought that the Indians are brooding in their slow, silent way, and that some day a terrible outbreak will take place on Ometepec. In this sudden manner all the great movements of the race are made. They are a people singularly patient, thrifty, and laborious; little inclined towards violence, but indomitable in defence when once they have taken arms. It was the Indian soldiery whose stolid resistance overcame the dashing valour of the filibusters.

A sister peak, Zapatero, once densely inhabited, now contains one house only, the residence of the vacquero in charge of the cattle herds. Both Ometepec and Zapatero contain considerable remains of the early Indian races, and we shall speak of them more at length hereafter. Some writers on Central America would transform Zapatero, which signifies "cobbler"—the point of which designation certainly does not appear very clear—into "Zapotera," and derive the name from the Aztec "Zapotl," modern "Zapote," a fruit very common in Nicaragua. This is possible enough, but it is a mere conjecture. Besides these two large islands, there are numerous little rocks, most charming in their delicate verdure, scattered along the Chontales coast.

Before the filibuster war a good deal of trade was carried on, in the thriftless Creole fashion, over the lake. Vessels of ten and fifteen tons were common enough, and of schooners even larger there were not a few; but that war gave the country a blow from which, by its own exertions, it never can recover. So much mischief was done on either side in mere wantonness; forces so utterly disproportionate to the numbers of the population were raised and expended; the people became so demoralized, and ambitious men so used to power and lawlessness, that the overthrow of Walker cost the country, in blood and misery, a hundred times the price it might have paid in quietly remaining under his rule. We have nothing new to say about that leader, nor do we wish to repeat the balivernes of cheap patriotism. It *is* a hard thing to be under a foreign yoke, even though you may have voluntarily put yourself in such position; it *is* hard to see gigantic mercenaries striding about your streets, curse in mouth and revolver on thigh, without a struggle to regain your freedom; harder than all is it to hear your own sisters and cousins and sweethearts praising out loud the manly forms and fearless hearts of those rude barbarians who thrust you off your own pavement, and contemptuously address you to your face as a " dam Greaser." * Yet every

* This most expressive but unexplainable word is a legacy of the Mexican war. It was a contemptuous expression applied by the American soldiers to their enemy, and has since become common to all mongrel populations of the Spanish colonies. It is not used to Indians of pure blood, whom all respect as a hard-working, brave, and worthy race.

man among the upper classes of Nicaragua knew that those wild filibusters were but the forerunners of a new era for his country—an era of prosperity, of peace, of security. Had not the natives scowled, those big, good-hearted rowdies would have treated them kindly enough. It was no patriotism which roused the five republics to unite in driving out the handful of invaders. It was envy, and wounded vanity, and secret ambitions; and, on the part of some, a very dread of quiet and order.

When Walker was turned out and shot, poor fellow! under circumstances not quite sufficiently explained by our government, where was the patriotism of the Nicaraguan generals? Verily, the seven devils who came in then were worse than the one cast out. Walker's schemes for the regeneration of the country were not more grand than practical. What has since been done, save in fighting, and plunder, and intrigue? There is not a road in Nicaragua; there is not a manufacture; there is not a vessel of twenty tons on lake, river, or ocean; there are no exports, except hides and natural produce, in proportions absurdly small to the fertility of the country; there are no schools; there is not a bank; the postal service is a practical joke. What is there besides bigotry, and turbulence, and vice?

We left San Carlos in the evening, and before sunrise reached the neighbourhood of San Miguelito. I went on shore with the mate, to the point where the stores and machinery of the Consuelo Gold Company are landed; and we found there piles of iron and heaps of boxes, which had been left two months previously: they were not removed, owing to the impossibility of transport. I believe that Captain Paul, who is in charge of the works at Consuelo, has since made a practicable road to this place; but at that time the only communication was by a path as wide as a cart-rut and as deep as a river. In the afternoon we reached the old fort of Granada, a picturesque pile of ruins, standing upon a foundation of rough stone, about a hundred yards in the lake. The shore was crowded with bathers, and washerwomen, and idlers. High-born caballeros were standing, stark naked, beside their little Arab horses, washing them down. Close by, a group of men, apparently engaged in the repair of a canoe, was picturesque in the same simplicity. Women of every age, from the white-haired granddam to the baby, were splashing about in utter innocence. Children were rolling their wet bodies in the deep sand. Groups of horsemen were dashing about, at the quickest amble of their small steeds. It was the liveliest scene we saw in the country, except during the earthquakes.

The boat was beached beside the machinery of a steamer wrecked here some months before. None of the bathers paid much attention to our party, except by a long stare at the strangers. The women were all shockingly ugly, coarse and heavy in feature, and thickset in figure. I am willing to believe there may be beauties among the Spanish Creoles, though I never saw one; but the negro and Sambo blood in Nicaragua has ruined the good looks they may once have had. Possibly, if the women were better looking, they would not be so liberal with their "points." This idea struck us at the moment, and we subsequently found it true : the girls with any pretensions to good looks bathed in the less exposed situations, or did not bathe at all.

Granada is the oldest city in Central America. It was founded in 1562,* upon the site of a large Indian town; and while Nicaragua was under the rule of Spain, this settlement thrived notably. At present, ruin and dirt and stagnation abide unchecked in all its borders. General Henningsen, the hero of the filibusters, blew up the churches and burnt the town in 1856, and little has since been done to restore its prosperity. The houses of the better class are of one story, built round a courtyard; their material is mud, shaped into gigantic bricks, and covered with smooth plaster. The windows are usually bowed in shape, unglazed, but protected by iron bars. Ceilings are quite unknown; and any one so luxurious as to require a floor must put up with earthenware tiles. The furniture is simple in the extreme, generally consisting of a hammock and half a dozen unpolished chairs, with a table of rough wood. Two or three pictures of saints —who must have been meritorious, they are so ugly—a disgusting crucifix with lots of tinselled rubbish about it, are the only decorations on the

* The first city of Granada was built by Hernandez de Cordova, two years after the conquest in 1524.

bare whitewashed walls. The bedrooms contain a framework of heavy posts, on which a bull's hide is stretched, over that a mat, and then a blanket or two. There are, I believe, one or two families which boast a pair of sheets, but we did not see any. This, the reader will bear in mind, is the furniture of a well-to-do family. Among the poorer classes an inventory becomes much simpler. Take from the above everything except the hammock; make the saints more hideous, and, I suppose, more efficacious; add millions of vermin and "neguas." Nevertheless, all classes consider themselves on a giddy pinnacle of luxury, and the priests are continually reminding them of the share of wealth they owe to the church.

There are about ten native houses in Granada in which can be found a few articles of ornament which we should call primitive in Europe, such as a tablecloth, an arm-chair, a cabinet.

We walked about half a mile over a sandy road, in which the rains had made ruts two to three feet deep, and reached the church of Guadaloupe, which General Henningsen, with four hundred men, defended against four thousand Central

American troops. The city is built upon successive platforms, raised some eight feet one above the other, and ascended by quaint inclines of rough pavement. These curious works are remains of the Spanish dominion, and no one attempts to keep them in repair : if a pebble give way or fall out, the hole remains unfilled. The lake road itself was rapidly growing up at the time of our first visit. Further and further, with each month, the flowering shrubs pushed their branches over the pathway, and a carpet of blue convolvulus formed more thickly under foot. Before we left, however, the municipality sent twelve convicts, under charge of twenty-four soldiers, to clear away the jungle and reopen the road.

We reached the only hotel, kept by Mons. Mestayer, a Frenchman, about five o'clock in the evening,—too late for dinner. The laws of the Medes and Persians were not more unchangeable than are the customs of Nicaragua ; but, on the other hand, it is probable they were more in accordance with common sense. Our host was full of good-will; he shouted and swore at the domestics ; he got red in the face and tore his white hair ; but to what purpose ? One dinner only per diem was down in the bond of his Indian cook; and no bribe, no threat of earthly punishment, could have overcome the senseless routine of that flabby old woman. "I can give you no dinner, messieurs, but there is some cold meat; you must do with that. Sacré Dieu! Quel pays abominable!" It had a peculiar flavour, that cold meat; a suspicion of garlic hung over it; and any possible jury would have pronounced it guilty of tallow and cinders, and that odd taste we used to call "native sauce" in the East. With this simple repast we drank an abomination, a horror, called Chateau Margaux, which tasted like the waters of the Garonne after vine harvest. Also there were cold yams, pumpkins, and raw tomatoes. We feasted like caballeros of Nicaragua.

The repast was served up in the courtyard, under the verandah. All around us were parrots, and macaws, and paroquets, and orioles, and rabbits, and pigeons, and partridges. The birds, except the last, sat upon pegs nailed to the pillars, and screamed with a strength of lung reminding us of certain philharmonic performers in the land of our affection. There was one immense macaw, dressed with very bad taste in a scarlet jacket and hood, with blue train and sleeves, which made a noise "like a dry millwheel in flood time, only more so," as one of our American friends remarked. He doubled himself forward, "like a virtuous deacon a-snikerin' out the sins of those he don't jine to in his connection," and screamed with a will. The parrots took up the chorus, and even the pretty little paroquets chirped quick and shrill, adding their mite to the disturbance. When our meal was finished we surveyed the hotel.

On the side next the street it was a store, and one of the largest in the town. From millinery to patent medicines, every want of a Nicaraguan could be supplied there; and if the assortment was not very luxurious, it was at least fitted to the customers. Passing through the store, one emerged in the courtyard, which was surrounded by a verandah on which the bedroom doors opened. The centre was occupied by a square of ground, laid out in a primeval age as a garden for flowers and fruit; but the plants, following that law of progress which even the Nicaraguans cannot arrest, had long since run wild, and now thrust up great spears and spikes of withered blossom. Beyond this large courtyard was a second, of which the stables and cookhouse occupied two sides. The stable was a very simple idea, its appointments being merely a few rings fastened to the wall, to which the mules and horses were attached. Great fights they used to have sometimes; but the animals of Certral America are much more peaceful than those of better-regulated countries—I suppose they profit by observation of their masters.

This was the hotel. The dining-room was the verandah; the sitting-room was one's own bedroom; the cellar was the back shop, and the kitchen was a hole. But all honour to Mons. Mestayer, our delightful host! Whatever could be done in that thriftless town to secure the comfort of a traveller, he did with all his heart; and the amount of bad language expended in our service merits and receives eternal gratitude. In vain we reminded him of his latter end, and entreated moderation in the expression of his views. All was useless; but the memory of our efforts still thrills us with conscious virtue.

He said he had lived five and twenty years in Nicaragua, and feared no future fate.

Nearly opposite the hotel stands a wonderful building of " adobes,"* somewhat resembling the mud pie of infancy, constructed on a model of the Tower after the great fire. This imposing edifice, which is quite adequate to support an attack of popguns, is the fort, the police court, and the Government House. Its front occupies a large portion of the Plaza; and when the two sentries, with bare feet, grey uniform, and straw hats, are strolling up and down before the entrance, it presents an aspect of magnificence which strikes dumb the stranger and awes the disaffected. Occasionally an officer passes in or out, upon which the sentries shut their eyes, spread wide their legs, present arms, and knock their hats off. Other barefooted soldiers, sitting under the archway, rush forward like one man, and replace the hats on their heroes' heads. At night these sentries become very grand. After

---

* Adobes are big bricks of mud and hay, two feet in length by eighteen inches in breadth and one foot in thickness. The word is the Egyptian " adaub," and was carried into Spain by the Saracens. From thence it came to America.—Jarvis, " Scenes and Scenery in the Sandwich Islands."

eight o'clock every individual crossing the Plaza, or walking in any of the streets within sight, is challenged with much ferocity: "Kur-r vie-ee?" which stands for "Quien vive?" "La Patria!" "Kay-ay Hen-ent?" which stands for "Que gente?" "Gente de paz!" This ought to be the conversation exchanged between the vigilant sentry and the belated wanderer; but when the vigilant sentry addresses his proud challenge to a tall citizen of the States, he rarely gets any other answer than "Americanos, d—— you!" or, worse still, a fierce growl of "Greaser!" And with this the poor fellow has to be content. Next time the simple native comes under his eye, how he suffers for the insolence of the "Macho!" How he is bullied about his business and his residence, his godfathers and godmothers, and Church Catechism generally. They are pretty quick with their "gas-pipes," too, these rude soldiers, when the suspicious party is not of European blood.*

Next to the Presidio is a large church, com-

* Throughout Central America a foreigner in all societies is called a "Macho," or he-mule. It can scarcely be a wonder if he return this compliment by an unsparing use of that suggestive epithet, "Greaser."

pletely ruined by General Henningsen, before his evacuation of the town. Certainly no one can excuse, or in any way palliate the wanton mischief worked by the filibusters when they found themselves unable to hold their ground; and the destruction of Granada was the grossest of all these cases. Any one who knows the Central American Creoles can understand and sympathize with the mad humiliation felt by those hot-blooded Anglo-Saxons on feeling themselves overpowered by the multitude of the enemy; but many of the most unjustifiable outrages were ordered and carried out by those superior officers whose self-command should have restrained the excesses of their men. Nevertheless, we calm spectators should make allowance for hot blood; and towards its close the war was carried on in the simple fashion of Central America—no quarter. It is due also to the filibusters to note that this barbarism was brought into the struggle by the cruel soldiery of Honduras and Guatemala.

I must do General Henningsen the justice to observe that he destroyed some of the very ugliest buildings in the world. Whether we regard the tottering ruins of ten churches still unrepaired, or whether we examine the rebuilt seven, the mind must still refuse to conceive a model more hideous, more disproportionate, and, at the same time, more insignificant. In vain is the heavy façade built up between two square towers. In vain is a big round window pierced through the centre, like a gigantic O! of disgust. In vain is whitewash and stucco besomed in, and windows, round and square and oblong, disposed in the intervals. Notwithstanding these adornments, the effect is incredibly poor and ugly. Would he had blown them all up, beginning with that colossal altar of deformity, the cathedral at Leon! Seventeen large churches to a population of ten thousand! Even in England the proportion would be immense; but the custom of the Roman Church, which disposes of its followers in various lots throughout the morning, makes the superfluity absurd. But to the Central Americans the "egglesia" is a substitute for all other amusement. When the worshippers are a little tired of their favourite preacher—it *is* difficult to be original in the pulpit, isn't it?—they go and criticize the performances at other shrines, and try the efficacy of a new saint. In the eternal nature of things, if man have no legitimate amusement, he will make one out of any public ceremony that may be at hand; witness the branding oxen and the dipping sheep in Australia, both of which disagreeable operations are great fêtes to the population.

The country round Granada is volcanic in the extreme. The great mountains of Mombacho, on one side, and Masaya, on the other, are only distant about three leagues, and the latter is still in activity. The town is half encircled by a deep fissure of volcanic origin, used in some parts as a road. Two of the suburbs are cut off by this immense ditch, which in many places reaches a width of a hundred feet, and a depth of sixty, with banks as steep as a wall, and overgrown with many-coloured weeds. Along this covered way Walker marched his hundred and seventy-five filibusters, who carried Granada by storm and raised the siege of Guadaloupe church. Looking down into the matted depths of this ravine—depths untried and seemingly impenetrable—and then turning to the thin, bare walls of the besieged church, the glory of either party seems to be equal. To enter that unknown crevasse at midnight; to cut a road through the snake-twined undergrowth; to risk the danger of hidden fissures, of falling rocks, of deep morasses, and mud quicksands, all in a pitchy darkness, required moral as well as physical courage. Discovery was almost certain, when every man must have died, helplessly buried in the mass of earth and stone pushed down from above. But they were not discovered; they scaled the precipice by Otrabanda; they dashed down the main street; they stormed three barricades; forced the intrenchments of an enemy twenty times their number; drove him, broken and panic-stricken, from the town, and set free General Henningsen and the band of two hundred heroes who still defended a heap of ruins. There is no need to compare the bravery of these men.

The population of Granada is almost entirely Mestizo, or Mulatto, or Sambo. The first name expresses the mixture of white and Indian blood, the second, white and negro, the third, Indian and negro. European fashions have been adopted here, as elsewhere, to the uprooting of national costume; but the women still keep the loose camice, or chemisette, which leaves the neck and shoulders bare. Nevertheless, upon great occasions they lace themselves in stuffy dresses, high up to the throat and long in the sleeves, which must cause them a martyrdom. In feature all are very plain, and their voices are harsh and disagreeable. Negro blood is so widely rooted, that its characteristics are constantly breaking out among children of all ranks; and in a family of fair complexions and straight hair, will be found a little mulatto, showing the blot of five or six generations back. The mental qualities of the Granadinos are the curse of the country. Their turbulence, pride, and jealousy, have caused the ruin of their town and the slow retrogression of their native land. Granada is the seat of the aristocratic, anti-foreign party, while its rival, Leon, is the headquarters of the democratic, or progressive party. These two towns have sacked one another again and again without in any way settling the questions at issue. The fact is that Granada wishes to destroy Leon, and Leon to destroy Granada; and thus no progress is made towards consolidation, and no progress ever can be made. It is a mistake to suppose that the Spanish Indians are, as a body, turbulent. On the contrary, no country could desire a more peaceful, industrious class of labourers than is the agricultural population of Nicaragua; and a stranger is puzzled to know how the many revolutions, which prove such a curse to the country, are brought about, when these people abstain from anything like even agitation.

"The fact is, that every revolution effected from Chili to Mexico is brought about by such a mere fraction of the population, that it seems a wonder to an Englishman that the great majority do not arise and speak out. . . . But they do not speak out, nor do they act; and the consequence is, that they are plundered, robbed, and murdered in the most shameful manner by the small minority of rascals. But they half deserve it; for if the nine, or the ninety and nine, would make the protest, they would have a very small percentage who would back their protest by an appeal to arms, even in defence of their homes and families.

"In Central America every State has a small number of soldiers, ill paid, worse fed and clothed, and of the lowest order of scoundrels; the officers being hardly a shade better, but with a little more method in their general conduct. Leon, being the capital of the department of Nicaragua, and head-quarters for the troops,* may contain fifty thousand inhabitants and about three hundred dissolute soldiers; and it is by this mere handful of ruffians that revolutions are effected. A subaltern officer gains over a portion of the men with promises of plunder, increased pay, and promotion for the non-commissioned officers to the commissions soon to be vacant. They await the time when the barrack-guard and sentries will be all composed of men so gained over. The barracks are then taken possession of in the night, the Commandant's house stormed and plundered, and next morning a few volleys of musketry make people acquainted with the fact that their late

---

* The work from which this extract comes was published in 1849. At the present day Leon cannot boast twenty thousand inhabitants, but it has more than three hundred soldiers. The remainder of the description is singularly true.

Commandant and his adherents have been placed on the fatal 'Banqueta,' and have made vacancies for the successful rebels, who may most likely be destined to suffer the lex talionis in a few months.

"Armed parties are then sent round to every house, to gather forced contributions, in the name of the new government, from all parties, but very especially from those who are known to be favourable to their predecessors. Those that will not, or cannot pay, are dreadfully ill-treated; they are often taken out and shot before their families, and their houses, stores, or shops ransacked of everything not too hot or heavy to carry off. These revolutions are likewise excellent opportunities for the most depraved (generally allied to the soldiery) for a general plunder, and too often enables them to satisfy their revenge for former affronts or quarrels. . . . . The reason for these émeutes is as mysterious as the refrain of the old song—

> 'Friends and foes,
> To battle they goes,
> But what they all fight for, nobody knows.'

Like many other agitations, they are invariably

got up for the personal profit of a few at the expense of the great majority." *

Read the despair of the natives themselves shown in a Government report made to the Chamber of Deputies in 1853 : " Nada existe sino la experiencia de nuestra disgracia, pero una experiencia ciega que solo alimenta personalidades y localismos miserabiles, en donde vemos in pugna un hombre contra otro, una contra otra familia, un pueblo contra otro departemento, y con tal eteragenidad de interes jamás podra formarse de estas elementes un estado."—We have no experience, but the experience of our unfortunate petty local jealousies and personal enmities. From these come struggles between man and man, between members of the same family, between one town and another. With such contention of private interests a state can never be formed.

When we arrived, disturbances were expected daily. Tomas Martinez, the President, a man who had risen from a low rank to the highest office of the state, was suspected of an intention

* From " Wild Life in the Interior of Central America." By George Byam, pp. 16, 17, 18.

to cling to power beyond its legal term. In case he should not carry his re-election, he was believed to meditate a "pronunciamento." The leading men of Granada thought to oppose this by a counter "pronunciamento." Instantly springs the civil war. No complaints were to be heard against Martinez; he had kept peace during his time of office; ninety-nine of every hundred in the country wished his re-election, illegal though it might be. Yet at this moment, when every family in Granada was positively, comparatively, or superlatively ruined, the insignificant minority was preparing a new war. Verily the gods fool these people to their destruction.

Volcanic action has not yet ceased in the neighbourhood of Granada, though at the time of our visit folks had begun to forget the alarms of their youth, and to doze over the earthquake stories of their grandams. Good Faith! they had a rude awakening. On the south-west of the town are several round hillocks, which the observant Indians assert to be growing higher and more conical every year; of late this increase has, to their eyes, perceptibly quickened.

The fact is probable enough, being common in volcanic regions. Granada has suffered less from such convulsions than any other town in Central America, and now its turn seems at hand.

In the city itself there is nothing further to describe; it is but a heap of ruins. A municipality indeed there is, but we never could rightly distinguish it from the stables of a neighbouring house. A sort of dingy, dirty, candle-lit café there is, whither all the world goes in an evening to play cards for a few "dimes," and billiards "for a drink." At this café there is no coffee, and the only liquid procurable is bottled beer sent up from Greytown as damaged. Cockfighting there is on a Sunday, at which an "ounce" is staked now and then, and a few dozen birds are killed. Granada is a dream of desolation—a nightmare—a horror unspeakable. Politeness is indeed to be found among the upper classes, but hospitality is a virtue unknown or forgotten. We warn the intending traveller, as we were warned, that if any one offer him a glass of water, he had best feel if he have a "dime" about him before accepting it; payment will certainly be expected if not asked. Letters of introduction are a formality quite unnecessary; they are no possible good, and the travellers' friends are uselessly bored in getting them. Of course I do not speak of the foreign planters in Nicaragua ; *their* behaviour is always a credit to their country, whatever it may be.

The day after our arrival we went down early to bathe in the lake. A crowd of girls and children, washerwomen, horsemen, and bathers were there, as on the evening before, and we walked some distance over the beach before finding a decently lonely place. As to the natives, they all entered the water together in perfect innocence, and we were no doubt looked upon as haughty "machos," because we moved a little way out of the crowd. On our return, while standing in the doorway of the store, talking with the landlord, to us came limping Mr. A——, a six-foot-two American belonging to the Transit, who had slept in the hotel the previous night. When within hearing—
' Thunder !" he cried to Mestayer. " You keep all the luxuries of this polished country constant on tap, you do ! Cast a tender glance at that !"—

drawing off his boot and shaking a scorpion out of it. "Kind o' rough that, ain't it now? That scorpion has been stinging me for the last two hours, as venomous as an old maid at a wedding breakfast. Nor he ain't got his coffin measure yet, though I've stamped him as flat as a skating floor!"

Really and positively, Mr. A—— had been walking about the town all the morning with one of these horrid reptiles in his boot, stinging him from time to time. Fancy how he must have bullied the wretched natives with whom he had business! In the East a man would have pulled his boot off rather quicker than thought; but the American scorpion is not nearly so painful or dangerous. In colour it is a deep dull green relieved with purple, not so handsome as the black and white mottling of the Asiatic species, or the dusky transparency of the African. In size also it is much inferior to its fellows of our hemisphere.

We were detained ten days in Granada by a very serious complaint of Ellis's, and Heaven forbid we should ever go through such a martyrdom again! There was nothing to do from hour to hour and from day to day. The aristocracy keeps the shops, and there it dozes; middle classes there are none; the lower orders keep the Plaza, and there they doze. I really believe it is the hammock which has pulled down the active old Spanish spirit to its present stagnation. The national ensign of Nicaragua should be a hammock waving over a graveyard. For the people are dead, and their ghosts loll all day in the murderous net. You enter a house—there is the owner swinging in his hammock, undressed, unwashed, not reading, not working, not thinking. There he lies, with his children beside him, backwards and forwards gently swaying in a half-doze. Between his lips is the paper cigarette, near his hand is the jug of lemonade, but in his head there is not an idea, whether of virtue or vice. As you enter the open doorway he looks up languidly, motions you to a parallel hammock, offers you a light for *your own* cigarette—if you have not one he has none either—and there you may lie and swing so long as you may please. It is not necessary to make a remark during your visit; you are at liberty to do so, but the answer is so drowsy, so softly impregnated with hammock, that conversation is not encouraged. Nicaragua lies in its hammock all day and sleeps therein at night. When the general should be at the head of his troops, he is dozing in a gorgeous hammock of dyed grass; when the army should answer the call of the general, the army is swinging softly in its ragged hammock of twine. The merchant has a hammock in his counting-house; in the absence of customers he lies therein. The priest performs his parish duties suspended like Mahomet between heaven and earth; he longs for a dispensation to get through mass in a similar position. The doctor receives his patients, the lawyer his clients, the lady her lover, the deputy his constituents, the constituents their deputy, all lying in the devoted hammock. From his hammock the host greets his guests, the minister harangues the deputation, the general addresses his army, and the president consults his cabinet. To the hammock flies the lover in search of consolation; the disappointed candidate, the henpecked husband, the ruined storekeeper, all find their solace in the tender swing. Fields are cultivated in it, battles are won, books are written, reforms are introduced, education is spread, everything is changed, and Nicaragua takes a foremost place in the world's civilization. But when the well-meaning visionary leaps out to carry through these dreams, his back bends, his head swims, he sinks into his hammock and dreams again.

CHAPTER III.

Ellis's strange malady—Ascent of Mombacho—Start for Chontales —First camp—Catching an alligator—Booted and barefoot classes in Nicaragua—Geographical problem—A long forest ride—Shooting one's supper—Lassoing a bull—Nicaraguan roads—Casa Blanca—A tropical stream—Juigalpa—Amiable priest—Indian remains—Tomb-breaking—Tales of mystery—Uncanny behaviour of our Indian host—More tales of wonder—Great tombs—Portrait statues—Restoration—A dreary camp—Pumas—Catching a puma —A weary night—Garrapatas—Arrival at Libertad.

THE disease from which Ellis was suffering on our arrival at Granada was a mysterious swelling and blistering of the foot, which had broken out the day we left Greytown. Thin scarlet lines passed in zigzag under the skin, and each morning showed an increase of them, as if a worm had been at work during the night, making fresh burrows. None of the Americans or natives on board the steamer had ever seen or heard of a similar case, and we became not a little anxious before reaching Granada. In forty-eight hours after the first symptoms all sensation was lost in two toes, and we were in great dread of mortification—a result which would doubtless have happened in a few hours more. Dr. Flint, an American long settled in the town, pronounced it to be Guinea-worm, but he had never before encountered a case. His treatment was to open the zigzags with a lancet and rub iron in the incision. This instantly restored feeling in the lost toes, and for a week or two the swelling gradually subsided; but after a time the worm seemed to get casehardened, and resumed his vigour, attacking both feet. Ellis finally overcame the enemy with lunar caustic applied direct to the scarlet lines. From what I have heard of Guinea-worm in the East, where it is rare, I doubt whether Ellis was suffering from it; and I have been thus prolix about a matter of no great importance, as it turned out, because we suspect strongly that by his own exertions our groom managed to discover a bran-new disease—a feat the more creditable because so disagreeable. For a time the appearance of his foot was frightful.

I myself was struck down on reaching Granada, and Mr. Jebb took advantage of this enforced delay to make an ascent of Mombacho, the great volcano, now extinct, lying to the southward of the town. But at the outset he found difficulties. Independently of the vague superstition which, I think, surrounds every volcano in these half-Christian lands, Mombacho has a terrible reputation for the ferocity of its "tigers," which abound. The mountain has never yet been climbed, though a party of Frenchmen some two years since made circumstantial boasts of their success. With some difficulty Mr. Jebb found two mestizos willing to engage, and about two o'clock one sunny afternoon he left us on this adventure, accompanied by Mr. D—— and Sammy. Two hours' riding, through open jungle and small patches of cultivation, brought the party to a large hacienda, surrounded with ruins of indigo-vats. Here they alighted for a few moments, and then entered a stony path cut through a dank, dense forest. Here and there were piles of ruin, which the unwarned traveller might conceive to be Aztec cities, or Itzimayas, or Quiché will-o'-the-wisps, but which were recognized by Mr. Jebb for ruins of Spanish cultivation. Just at sundown they reached an ancient crater, full a quarter of a mile in diameter. In form it was almost as smooth as a basin, and the green sloping banks were dotted with little thickets and clumps of majestic timber. Over this circular savannah they trotted, flushing thousands of waterfowl which lay in the reedy shallows. At a little rancho, far-famed in Mombacho climbs, they camped for the night. The old Indian within made many excuses for his unwillingness to engage in another ascent, but a judicious flash of dollars overcame all fears, and he agreed to guide the party whithersoever they would.

In spite of the old man's warning, Mr. Jebb camped outside the hut. A lively night he had! The sleepless congos howled and drummed all round; pale, smooth-treading pumas grunted and caterwauled in the bushes; tigers roared upon the mountain side. With the first light he roused the party, and they started. A short climb of half a mile brought them to a clearing, where cultivation ceased. After that, the forest was so dense that the sky was not seen once during two hours' ascent, and in most places even the upper branches of the trees were hidden. The undergrowth, contrary to the usual case in Nicaragua, was denser than Mr. Jebb had ever seen it in the East, and the trees were of incredible girth. In about two hours from the clearing they struck the trail of Monsieur Tavernier's party, two years before. Shortly afterwards they reached a dry torrent-bed, up which they slowly climbed. After an hour of this weary ascent, Mr. D—— broke down, and was seriously ill. After resting with him a while, they proceeded, and in half an hour came to water. The banks closed in rapidly upon them, and the water grew deeper and deeper in the muddy reaches. When they could march no further in the river-bed, Mr. Jebb made three successive attempts to climb the precipice which walled them in on the left. Each time they fell back defeated. Then they tried to lasso a big tree, and this also failed. Finally, they took the right bank, and reached smooth ground again: the climbing of the bank occupied an hour and a half, pulling themselves up with knives and lassoes. The aneroid marked 3800 feet.

From this ridge they made for Monsieur Tavernier's summit, where was water; but on reaching the spot the pond was found to be dry. It was a small crater, about forty yards across, and thirty feet deep. M. Tavernier was three days in reaching this point, but he was still far from the real summit.

It was now about five o'clock, and they had been eleven hours on foot. Between the spot where Mr. Jebb stood and the real peak lay the deep ravine, deeper now than ever, through which they had made so much of their way. The water in it was now deep and foaming, probably feeding some smaller stream which they had passed on the left hand. To go further that night was impossible, and the Indians obstinately refused to fetch water. "Not for one thousand dollars, Señor, paid now on this spot." Mr. D—— also was so ill with over-exertion and weariness, that it seemed scarcely safe to expose him to the heavy mountain dews; so, after a fruitless attempt made by Mr. Jebb and the guide to find a crossing of the barrancas, they turned homewards. The highest point marked by the aneroid was 5200 feet, and Mr. Jebb considered the peak to be at least five hundred feet higher.

Mr. D—— told me that he made the descent "upon his head;" and Mr. Jebb, while confessing his own mishaps, confirmed this story. All the party were so utterly worn out that they could barely move their limbs; but Mr. D—— fell head over heels from the top of the mountain to the bottom (spoiling my best bowie knife, by the way, in his efforts to save himself). The sun sank while they staggered down; the twilight glimmered among the thick-woven trees, and the cold moonbeams glittered through before they regained the rancho. About seven o'clock they again struck water, and one and all lay down upon the bank, and in drinking fell asleep. Mr. D—— and one of the guides woke several times in severe sickness, but nothing more serious followed this bold attempt to climb Mombacho in a single day. Thirteen hours, without a break, they had been engaged in a climb the nature of which no one could appreciate who has not attacked a mountain in the tropics.

In descending next morning they struck several trails, and Mr. Jebb had some sport.

Here they found the trail of a beast "having a head like an ox and a body like a mule," which I subsequently encountered upon the opposite face of Mombacho. Puma tracks, of a very large size, they also found, and Mr. Jebb noted a noble specimen of the great white falcon, so rare in Central America. It was as large as those Icelandic giants we sometimes see. Spider monkeys he also observed, and this species we did not meet with afterwards. Birds and beasts abounded. Parrots were, of course, in flights, and toucans, but he did not see one of the yellow paroquets which Mombacho alone produces. About two o'clock the party regained Granada.

Ellis's foot was at length so far useful to him that he could wear a slipper and bear the stirrup. Accordingly, we prepared for a ride to Libertad, the capital of the north-easterly province, Chontales, in the vicinity of which are numerous relics of the ancient Indian races. But the difficulty of striking a bargain with any mule-owner was immense. Objection after objection had to be discussed and ventilated before we could get a direct answer as to price; and when it was arranged, as we thought, that the animals should be brought to the hotel at a certain hour, in point of fact nothing whatever had been settled. First, one of the mozos engaged was not a good man; then ten dollars strong a month per mule was not as much as Don Somebody Something had paid, for the same journey, to the muleteer's great-great-grandfather, shortly after the conquest; then the quantity of "sacate," or fodder, to be given each mule per day, had not been regulated; then the man did not positively possess so many animals,—and then—and then,— the whole thing over again. But one evening, thanks to an American friend, the necessary number—eight mules and one old white horse— made their appearance in the courtyard, after an amount of perspiration on our part which would have sufficed to set forth fifty special trains in England. The old horse was given to Mr. D——, who ingenuously confessed his seat in the saddle to be painfully unsafe, and we mounted four of the mules. Two of the remainder were for the mozos, and two for baggage. Every possible article required on a journey had to be carried with us. Rugs, mosquito nets, preserved meats, spirits, powder, pots, kettles, knives, forks, tea, and coffee. *Nothing* is to be obtained in the interior, not even meat.

About three in the afternoon we set out, in a cavalcade which aroused no little commotion in the hot and dusty streets. Perhaps, of the whole party, Mr. Jebb's appearance was the most truly artistic. From the crown of his "mushroom" hat to the soles of his long boots, there was not an inch of him which did not suggest the "remorseless brigand." When he first appeared before us in travelling costume, a singularly fit remark was made by a bystander. "'Ternal thunder!" he cried, "Captain Jebb looks like the virtuous Heerod, a-footing out on his dangurious raid down to Bethlehem." My own suit of leather gave me a superior air, not, I fancy, without its admirers; but no impartial eye could observe Mr. D—— in the saddle without feelings of the warmest enthusiasm, tempered with fears for his too daring limbs. Few of those perilous feats which awed our youth at the circus were left unattempted by our active secretary; and if his success was not always apportioned to his boldness, eternal honour should at least reward such undaunted perseverance. As the bystander judiciously observed, on seeing him pass, with one leg on the crupper of his steed, while the other half encircled his neck, " If that mirac'lus horseman could only stay in any of them superior positions just long enough to be photographed, the picture would fetch a might of money in the States, as a model skippin' Jack for babes!"

We had designed to make our first camp at El Paso; but the lateness of our departure, and a delay caused by the baggage slipping off in a hole, compelled us to bivouac before even reaching Los Cocos, where the Chontales road leaves the lake shore. The ride was exceedingly pleasant, between jungle and water. We camped early, in order to pursue our journey by moonlight. After a delightful supper of broiled ham and biscuit, we lay down upon the soft sand, and the mosquitoes claimed their prey. For my own part, I fell into a doze in spite of them, mainly enticed thereto by sentimental thoughts about my last bivouac on the other side the world, but our sleep was soon disturbed by a rumour that three of the mules had broken loose. Ellis it was who made this discovery, and we roused the mozos at once. Deeply they swore at the too sagacious conduct of their charge, but when we represented to them that the runaways were not likely to return for any amount of "carajos," they mounted, and set off in pursuit.

The moon was just peeping over the blue volcanoes, and casting a long beam across the lake, when the last faint " thud " of the mules' gallop reached our ears. It was about as lovely a scene as man could wish to behold. The sky was deeply, airily blue, as at noonday, and the feeble stars were quenched in the rising moonlight, as if their brilliancy had been drawn from them to swell the greater orb. Twenty yards from our camp was the dense line of forest, showing black and awful in the stillness, with funereal plumes of palm waving over it, and light branches rustling and sighing before the feeble breeze. At our feet the broad miles of water rippled delicately, like a silver net ; in their midst stood the twin peaks of Ometepec, glittering like steel on the topmost crags, dark and misty below ; beyond were the deep blue volcanoes of Costa Rica. The majestic silence was unbroken, save from time to time by the shrill cry of a night bird, or the mournful howl of a restless " congo." As these sounds died echoing away, the "lap" of the glittering waves could alone be heard.

I naturally wished to convey my impressions of this scene to some living creature, and having lighted a cigar, and hunted up a neat quotation from Byron, I looked round for Mr. Jebb, to let it off. But Mr. Jebb was not visible. Mr. D—— and Ellis were sleeping in the moonlight with that trying restlessness which the novice generally experiences for the first two or three nights of camp life; Sammy was snoring like a "congo" with a cold in its head; but Mr. Jebb was not visible. "An awful state of things this," I thought, as I sat down on a heap of loose articles to meditate upon the situation. "Either," I thought, "my friend Jebb has been carried off by an alligator, or devoured by a tiger, or else he is taking a stroll along the moonlit shore. In the two former cases it would be well to make ready the gloomy tear, in the latter it might be best to shout him. Whoo-oop!" I yelled, in my finest jungle falsetto. "Whoo-oop!" pealed over the water in instantaneous answer. I looked at the lake in consternation; no canoe was there, no island, nothing but water of unknown depth.

"It is the spirit of Mr. Jebb," I thought; "his body has been eaten by the alligator, but his indomitable soul answers me from the monster's jaws." "Halloo, there! Have the mosquitoes gone to roost?" "Not a bit of it," I replied. "If a shower came now, the water would drain through me like a sieve, their bites are so many and so deep." "I've been sitting up to my mouth in the lake for the last two hours, and three times have nearly caught an alligator. Come and join me." The situation was pretty, and rather romantic, but I did not care for catching alligators in that manner, so I lay placidly down again, and let the mosquitoes do their wicked will. But finding the quotation sit heavily upon my spirit, I let it off at Mr. Jebb, over the water, and he grunted.

The mules were recovered before daybreak, and we set forward for El Paso. For some few miles further the road followed the shore line, winding among tall bushes of acacia which tore our clothes to rags. The number of alligators was really fearful. They lay together as thick as tadpoles in a pond, and many times we might have counted five hundred in sight at once.

At Los Cocos we left the shore, and plunged into a scanty forest, scarcely more obstructed with underwood than is an English cover. The road was broad enough and smooth, there was little mud, and had we been pressed for time, we might have reached El Paso by eight o'clock; but the monkeys and the parrots and the big anthills, and the thousand other wonders of tropical nature, drew us continually from the road. Far different from eastern jungles, the animal life here was abundant. All sorts of creatures crossed our path, some new, some recognized as friends of former travel. The absence of that dense large-leaved bush, to which we had been used, enabled us to see far along the glades, but on the other hand, it took much away from the beauty of the scene. There was scarcely any foliage within our reach from the ground, and the general character of the forest was sticky in the extreme; a peculiarity no doubt owing to the metallic nature of the soil around Granada.

About eleven o'clock we reached El Paso, having lost each other several times in too earnest study of natural science. One of the mozos took upon himself to remark upon this leisurely mode of travel, and we found it necessary to bring him to order. This fellow, who was a fair specimen of the " booted class" in Nicaragua, had all the vices and impertinence of the Yankee servant, without one of his virtues. We kept him up tight enough, but his idle, insolent face was painfully irritating to Mr. Jebb and myself. We were delighted to see the last of him, for sometimes the inclination to strike that impudent countenance was almost irresistible; but he never gave us the chance. The other mozo was of the "barefoot class," and a capital fellow in every way. He stayed with us through all our Nicaraguan experiences, and a better or more willing servant one could not desire. He had much Indian blood, though his hair curled crisply, and the race especially showed itself in an eccentricity of humours. His general character was silent, careless, and apathetic, but the wildest merriment occasionally seized upon him, and these fits were usually in the most incongruous situations. A violent storm, a midnight ride over dangerous ground, or a dreary camp with nothing to eat or drink, always roused our Mark Tapley to intense vivacity.

At such times he broke into songs of wonderful nose power, told scandalous tales to his fellow-mozos, with great perception of dry humour, and laughed heartily at the most prosy circumstances. A handsome fellow, too, and of well-tried bravery, was our trusty mozo, Gulielmo.

There are only two classes of men in Nicaragua—those who wear boots, and those who go barefoot. This distinction is so thoroughly recognized, that no man claiming to be "booted" will ever make a public appearance barefoot, even though his boots be mere upper-leathers strapped over the instep. On the other hand, a "barefoot" will not wear boots unless he sees a probability of emerging permanently from the lower class. The prices of all entertainments are regulated accordingly—half-price for bare feet; and the actors themselves told us that the simple expedient of removing the shoes to save half the entrance money was never used. With the solitary exception of the Chamorro family, every man of wealth or birth in Nicaragua keeps a shop, whatever may be his other avocations; and this is the case throughout Central

America, except in Guatemala. All the booted class keep a shop, or have an interest in that of some one else ; therefore they are aristocratic. After all, if there must be distinctions of class, this seems to be a very proper line to draw, and it has the advantage of being easily recognizable. If we had such a simple system in England, there would be an end to that awful scandal which arises from time to time, when belted earls are mistaken for their own butlers, and noble dukes requested to get an ice. How they manage these things in Costa Rica, I will tell when we get so far on our travels.

El Paso is surrounded with small fields of tobacco and indigo and sugar-cane, hedged in with " pinuelas," or wild pineapple. The village consists of some twenty huts on either bank of the river, which is about nine hundred yards broad. At the ferry we breakfasted on ham and " frijoles." Fortunately, our own bread was enough to render us independent of the " tortillas," which, with " tasajo " and plantains, were all the people could give. " Frijoles " are simply small beans boiled soft, and then fried in oil. In respectable houses they are utterly tasteless, at least when foreigners dine there, but in the huts of the poor they are a delicacy beyond price. I am not cook enough to say what difference there may be in the preparation, but it is probable the respectable families wash out their frying-pans occasionally. " Tortillas" are bannocks of crushed maize, tasteless, and sodden; they fill the place of bread, which is a luxury unknown. " Tasajo" is the sun-dried beef at this moment being tried in England. As I observe differing opinions as to the best mode of cooking this article, I will mention the simplicity of native fashion. A stick is thrust through half a dozen "chunks," which are pushed bodily into the fire; after five minutes they are taken out, and the foreigner may eat if he can. I suggest a trial of this mode, which may be called à l'aborigène. I daresay the "tasajo" is just as nice so as in any other fashion; for the natives, who pass their lives in masticating it, should surely know the best way of preparation. It is true there are many things they *should* know, of which their ignorance is utter.

This river, or estero, of Titipapa is a geographical puzzle, which we regret vastly not to have solved. Every traveller seems to have taken it for granted that the broad shallow stream he saw before him communicated with the Lake of Managua, and certainly the people of the village do not undeceive any one. I do not find, however, that any writer positively asserts he has passed along it, and since our return to England, we have noticed that Mr. Squier, who did examine it, denies that there is any river at all. He says that two long estuaries approach each other on either side the land, but that four miles of solid rock divide their nearest points. " No water flowed through it now, although there were pools here and there in the depressions of the rock, supplied with water from springs or from the rains. Clumps of bushes were growing in the dry channel, and amongst them cattle and mules were grazing. I can readily believe that anciently, during the wet seasons, a small quantity of water found its way through this channel and over the falls, a mile below; but nothing is more evident than that no considerable body of water ever flowed here."* And yet

* "Nicaragua: its People, Scenery, etc.," by E. G. Squier. Vol. i., pp. 418, 419. First Edition.

Mr. Scherzer gives an accurate length of the river, sixteen miles, and estimates its average depth at four feet. There is an extraordinary mistake here. Every single traveller whose works I can find treats the river Titipapa or Panaloya as a great fact beyond all question, and takes it largely into account in his canal schemes. I regret excessively that, like every one else, we took it for granted that communication existed between the two lakes.

About one o'clock we got the ferry-boat into motion, and crossed the estero, which is shallow, but full of big fish. Our mules were made to swim across, and, as few of them liked it, so much time was lost in getting them over, that we were scarcely in the saddle before three o'clock. It was very hot, sitting on the bank in that tumbledown village, waiting for the animals. Close by the landing-place was a shrub so covered with large white blossom that not a leaf or a branch could be seen; it looked like a gigantic guelder-rose. In the midst of the bush sat a big black sow, wallowing in the undried mud of the last rains, and taking from time to time a great mouthful of the snowy flowers. Verily, we thought, a fit emblem for the country.

At El Paso we left the sandy region and plunged into the mud. The forest grew over a quagmire; the streams scarcely could flow, they were so heavy with dirt; the mules were up to their knees in stiff black mud. After four hours of filthy riding, we reached a hacienda, with no worse accident than half a dozen soft falls upon the part of Mr. D——. The women were polite here, but they held out no hope of rest. Beyond this inhospitable building was a broad river, which we forded in water almost over our mules' backs. Darker and darker grew the forest. The damp odours of decay which rise at nightfall began to thicken round; the monkeys' call became more dreary, the pale mists curled up, and the black trees rustled, and sobbed, and sighed before the night wind; but water must be found, and food for the mules, before we could camp.

In another hour we reached Malacotoja, where the currish people refused us food and shelter. For the last we cared not a jot; for the first, after offering any amount of money, we told them simply we should take it; and thrusting revolvers in our belts, went to the nearest house, gun in hand. There, as expected, we found fowls roosting in the trees, and the owners, seeing they must defend their poultry with their own bodies, consented we should have one white chicken which was sitting on a low bough. This was not likely to suit our wants; but I dimly discerned a black mass upon the bough above that devoted fowl, and throwing myself on the ground, to get the two birds in line, I fired and brought both down. This was not in the bond, but the owners took it quietly enough. Mr. Jebb, seeing a fat duck waddling past in great alarm at the firing, gave him a sudden cut with a bowie-knife, which decapitated him as neatly as possible. This also was arranged, and we parted capital friends.

Within a quarter of an hour the birds were plucked and on the fire all together, with potatoes, spoilt bread, and plantains. Then we rigged up the mosquito-curtains, set on the kettle for coffee, and smoked the festive pipe until the stew was suspected to be ready. Mr. D—— was head cook, and capitally he performed this duty; but

Ellis proved to be a neat hand at a beefsteak, and Jebb and I had impressions about such things. The birds were a little tough, but we ate like wolves, not being yet used to a fast of eight or ten hours. Then, after the pipe of thanksgiving, we turned in; but our curtains were much too large in the mesh, and besides, the light of our great fire shining through must have drawn the mosquitoes in: wherever one of these torments can see light through your curtains, he will crush through the mesh somehow. Poor Mr. Jebb had no sleep again that night; he sat in the smoke all the time. Mr. D—— and Ellis were too tired to keep awake, but their hands and foreheads were much swollen in the morning.

We started at sunrise, following a long hedge of pinuella, or wild pineapple, which enclosed large fields of tobacco. Then we struck a broad muddy river, and rode some distance along its banks, until, having outrun the mozos, we lost ourselves. Presently a shanty full of women and dogs, all very ugly, was reached, where we were informed that the mozos must pass shortly. Here Mr. Jebb shot the largest iguana

I ever saw: he was over eight feet long, and thick as a man's thigh; his colour was red, and he was certainly not of a common species. When our men came up, we bade farewell to all friends at the shanty, and went on through the forest, pursued by a drawling cry of "Adio-o-os, Seño-o-ores!" After an hour's ride, up to our girths in mud from time to time, we reached a creek which it was necessary to ford. The first step of Mr. Jebb's big mule took him into the mud up to his knees, and he refused to go further. A desperate back plunge for retreat, which few horsemen would have cared to sit, carried him in up to the girths: finding Mr. Jebb immovable, and the position somewhat worse than before, he began to think over his proper course, to smell the mud, and to look from side to side, in the wonderfully sagacious way a mule has. Finally he settled that the mud was not deep enough to smother him, and his best course was straight on. Suddenly shooting forward with the whole force of his powerful hind-quarters, he battled with the quagmire with all four feet at once, set every muscle of his body, and finally, after five minutes' struggle, dashed out into mid-stream, showing an activity, a power of sustained endurance, and a downright pluck, which few horses could have surpassed. Ellis himself after this admitted that mules were not such despicable animals as, in the pride of his Yorkshire heart, he had deemed them.

We all got across safely; but the baggage animals, in spite of shouts and blows and encouraging cries, were not so fortunate. One foundered entirely, getting too far from the line, and in her agonized struggles threw off her load. Everything was recovered, by swimming for it, but the delay of drying powder and instruments kept us an hour and a half on the spot. While we were so engaged, a mounted vacquero came up, leading a wild bull by a lasso round his horns. When the furious animal saw us he prepared to charge. The Indian, who sat at some ten yards distance, still as a statue, gave a sudden turn of the wrist, scarcely strong enough, as it seemed, to affect the bull in any way. Quick as thought, the great beast was thrown headlong, his horns being, I verily believe, the first part of him to touch ground. So incredible was the force of this fall that he never made a movement while we stayed, but lay prostrate in the brushwood. I have seen some feats of strength and skill, but never any to compare with that of the statue-like vacquero.

Riding past the body of the bull, we pushed on for Masapa, where we hoped to stay the night. A few miles more took us out of the muddy region into a stony, mountainous district, in which the trees were scattered in picturesque copses. Hitherto our road had been a cleared track through the forest, full of dangerous mudholes, but practicable for some months of the year to the strong bullock-waggons of the country. From this point the traveller may find his way as he best pleases, the Camino Reale, or King's Highway (!), lessening to a six-inch mule-track. The mud however disappears, excepting here and there, and in its place a difficulty arises for nervous riders, in the precipitous beds of rock which must be ascended or descended every ten minutes. However, mules are not less sure-footed on rock than in mud, and after the first day, a traveller will find himself going up or down precipices which, forty-eight hours before, he would have pronounced utterly impracticable. Understand that I speak of the *one highway* of Chontales. If, in defiance of advice from the natives themselves, a stranger should venture into one of the by-paths leading to Indian villages, or out-of-the-way cattle-farms, then may his heirs array themselves in mourning and spoil his goods. If he be not mercifully drowned in a river, he will certainly be smothered in a mud-hole, or smashed into little bits over a precipice.

Climbing continually, we reached the hacienda of Masapa about four o'clock, where we found a gentleman who spoke English, having been educated at Stoneyhurst. He told us that the wife of the proprietor was lying dead in the house, for which reason we could not be received: at Casa Blanca, he added, two leagues further over the mountain, we should find comfortable accommodation. Tolerably wild we were; and some other travellers present, who had been equally disappointed, hinted aloud their doubt of the story. Night would soon be settling down, and a ride in the dark over such a road made us all feel grave. After resting the mules half an hour, we set out again. It must be borne in mind that hospitality was not asked for at any of these haciendas—*that* was out of the question. We merely required fodder and provisions, at our cost, and to this we had a right, as at any other inn. However, in face of the excuse offered, nothing could be done; and we mounted again, in a humour little less murderous than the night before. In crossing a belt of wood, a St. Thomas' negro made his appearance, and walked beside us. He inquired very eagerly after Captain Bedford Pim, and desired us to inform him that the hotel he had formerly kept had been washed away bodily, and that Captain Pim must not rely upon again securing its sumptuous accommodation. This negro said he had been a lieutenant in the Mexican war, a colonel in the Nicaraguan army, and a free fighter all round since peaceful times set in: he guided us through the wood to the foot of Casa Blanca hill. The road became dreadfully bad soon after; but, though knowing we had lost our way, we still clambered on over rocks that none of us would have cared to face in a less reckless humour, and at length, just as darkness fairly set in, came out on the table-land of Casa Blanca, where was rest for the sole of our foot, and a better provision for comfort than at any other station in Chontales.

The supper was so admirable—that is to say, the frijoles were so good—that we determined to stay over the next day, to give Ellis's foot a little rest, and to break the monotony of our ride. This place also is famous for the number and daring of its " tigers ;" and our host had a pack of big dogs trained to this hunting. Some of them were beautiful animals—tall, deep-chested descendants of the Spanish bloodhound —but none could show purity of race. This was probably no misfortune in tiger-hunting. One great fellow, nearly as big as a mule, took such a fancy to me as to lie on my rug at night, and when I drove him off came back and licked my face. He was dark-grey in colour, very fine-limbed and deep-jowled, and would have been a valuable dog anywhere. He was being broken-in to tiger-hunting for a neighbouring " rico."

In the morning Mr. Jebb and I went out with dogs and men, but shot nothing worthy of special note. Then we went to bathe in a lovely mountain stream, as like a Westmoreland burn, overgrown with osmunda, as a scene in the glorious tropics can resemble a scene in sober England. The shallow, sparkling water, the feathery shadows, and the purple, moss-grown rocks were there; but how different was all else! In place of the osmunda were great tree-ferns, soft and delicate beyond all comparison of plumes; in place of bracken were tufts of feathery bamboo; every branch was decked with a fringe of orchids, and long trails of climbing moss fell in a green sweep from the tree tops.* Here a forest palm thrust out its head among the lighter foliage that walled in the stream; there a flowering shrub blazed in scarlet or gold. No sober linnets or grey finches drank at our stream; our birds were bright as the flowers, and varied as the leaves. Parrots in every possible mingling of green and blue and yellow and crimson; restless jays with azure wings; macaws brilliant as fire; and nameless birds that flashed from rock to rock on wings of prism. The water-spiders which sought their prey upon our burn were sparkling carbuncles. Our very

* On the Serebpiqui we saw this moss, which is very common in English greenhouses, falling in one mass from trees a hundred feet high. Another traveller, besides ourselves, has gone over that route and raved about it, as I know I shall when I get so far.

lizards were more beautiful than the brightest thing that lives in temperate zones. How they raised their tall red crests, and swelled their purple throats, as we passed beneath the boughs, slyly twisting round their glittering bodies, and leaving to our sight only the straining claws and the vigilant, glassy eyes. What if the stream were haunted by venomous fish and deadly water-serpents? What if the loveliest flowers were scentless, and the gay birds dumb? that vine-twisted thicket a tiger's den, and that soft moss a nest of snakes? Why, here is the very protest of Nature against the folly of our boasted age. The scorpion wars upon it with ready sting; the flower-gems scornfully give it the lie in their scentless beauty; the sleek panther yawns over it, and stretches forth his murderous claws for a testimony. Not yet, oh age of lead! are all things dull, and good, and uniform, and ugly! Still there are fierce strengths that bear no meddling, and useless beauties that glory in themselves, and gay heretics who laugh your dull faith to scorn! Shall the whole world become hideous because Manchester preaches utility, and Exeter Hall proclaims its crusade against strength and loveliness? Verily, no!

Some millions of sad centuries ago—the vulgar count it only two thousand, or twenty-five hundred years—they would have built a temple in this glen, in honour of the white-limbed hamadryads. For all the earth was then sacred to beauty, and man bowed down in worship before his own glory. He was proud then of his manhood; he prayed to gods of his own likeness, and knew, and boasted himself, a little lower than the angels. Shall we never more behold " that brightness of the world's eye," " those delicate days and pleasant," which once man saw? Never more! The iron is in all human souls, and not one among us can escape. But what a world was that which passed away two thousand years ago! What glory of intellect, what perfect beauty, what nobility of manhood was on this earth before one learned to pray for deliverance from the " lusts of the flesh, and the lusts of the eyes, and the pride of life!" Lusts! Look out the word in an old dictionary; it is rendered " delight—pleasure." Conceive it, oh you dead old Greeks! that men should pray to be excused from the pleasure of their eyes, and the strength of the life that is in them! Not such was your philosophy. Not so did you learn to paint, and carve, and speak, and write, as never man has since essayed. Not with such training did you climb the highest peaks of science, nor go forth to conquer at Marathon.

To what has our emasculated philosophy led us? To what, but meanness and ugliness and infinite littleness? I declare that no savages are so desperate to look upon as the run of folk one meets in every street. What else, in the name of Hephæstus—the ugly god, whose ugliness carries a moral—could be expected after two thousand years of " deliverance " from beauty?

The matter is too hopeless for discussion; besides, the Greeks, our masters, sought to convert no one. I lie open, patent, to a charge of Paganism; and, for aught I know, to more dreadful charges still. The Catechism is a mighty engine of commonplace invective. By the law of this England, statute, common, and canon, no man shall speak against its philosophy under a penalty of weak sneers and idiotic frowns; yet these, too, may be braved—almost with impunity, it is found. Man must protest for the faith and knowledge that is in him; laughingly if he can, vehemently if he must. But indeed there is little left in this dead world —little, at least, of sentiment and ethics—worthy of a struggle on the part of the elect. Once, to sit by that tropical brook, and dream over its beauty, must have roused the witness to noble thoughts and noble fancies; now, in this world they have deformed, it simply makes him feel cynical. For the order of the age is too strong for us.

Next morning we started early for Juigalpa, much better prepared to encounter the hardships of the road, and the annoyances of the people, by our day's rest at Casa Blanca. We were really comfortable there. Of course no one will think there were beds, or luxuries of any sort; much the contrary. We slept in the open air, upon the bare rock, exposed, at that elevation, to all the winds of heaven; but very little any of us cared so long as mosquitoes were absent. There was fresh meat, too, for we killed a young pig, and had him roasted whole. Try tasajo and tortillas, for forty-eight hours, oh dweller in Pall Mall! and then change to young "peccary;" afterwards state your sensations.

The road towards Juigalpa wound among volcanic hills, some of which had craters full of water. The valleys between were sometimes green savannah, sometimes bare rock, and sometimes, in the lower depths, great fields of dry mud, cracked and widely gaping with the heat. Countless herds of oxen, labouring through in the rainy season, had trampled them rough as lava-beds. They were most disagreeable riding, and not a little dangerous in the dark. Almost the only vegetation of these valleys is the "jicara," or wild calabash tree, which thrusts out strange rectangular branches, tufted over with a curious party-coloured parasite, looking like stained horsehair.* From the rectangular branches spring leaves, rectangularly, in sets of four, which form a cross; and for this reason the jicara is regarded with some superstition by the Indians, who call it Santa, or Santa Cruz

---

* I believe this strange parasite belongs to the *Bromeliaceæ*. Besides the curious hair-like leaves of scarlet and green, it bears a flower of pale crimson, very like a cactus, with purple centre. This flower is as large as the whole of the plant, and is very beautiful. Every twig bore one of these parasites.

Jicara. The wild fruit is of little use for calabashes, and to eat is poisonous. Cattle of a very large and handsome breed were in droves. Certainly, with all our care and expense, we have not in England any oxen or cows to compare with these wild herds. They paid very little attention to us, scarcely staring even when we jumped over them as they lay in the narrow path. Once or twice we met a herd, driven by the vacqueros to their corral, and then it was necessary to be cautious. The old bulls took the front in a solid line, crashing through the thickets, and breaking down the smaller trees, like a herd of elephants. Straight on they dashed, turning aside for no obstacle, but keeping down in the lower land. Behind were the half-savage vacqueros, mounted on small, active horses, and hurrying the maddened herds by unearthly cries and thrusts of a long goad.

Many of the volcanoes were little bowl-like elevations, from a hundred to a hundred and fifty feet high. They were perfectly smooth and round, covered with fine grass, and unbroken by any bush. Others there were of greater height, and all round the horizon were chains of lofty hills. Behind the highest lay Libertad and the gold country. A growing scarcity of trees was a peculiar feature of the scene. Already we had left the forest far behind, and bare tracts of green, covered with mountain grass, and destitute of flowers, lay all round us. Bushes and trees grew in long hedges by the frequent streams, and here and there was a hill crowned with a graceful copse; but in the valleys little timber was to be seen. Deer were tolerably plentiful.

At about seven o'clock in the evening we reached Juigalpa, after being thirteen hours in the saddle. Not a house or a human being had been seen since leaving Casa Blanca. It may be well to observe that wherever we passed a hut or a village I have mentioned the fact: this will give the reader a fair idea of the population of this province. Juigalpa, the second town of Chontales, has about eight hundred inhabitants, in a state somewhere about as low as they could possibly be for salvation. The houses are similar to those of the poorest class at Granada; but, in place of tiles, they are thatched with water-flags. We rode into the dirty plaza, in which was a dirty white church, a dirty store, and a filthy presidio. From this central point four streets descended, of which it was difficult to say which was most squalid. With some trouble we found a "hotel," where Captain P—— was accustomed to put up. The accommodation offered by this superior mansion consisted of one room and one bed among five of us. Fortunately there were three hammocks, and all the party except myself had long since become fond of this swinging couch. Accordingly the bed was ceded to me; Mr. Jebb took possession of one hammock, Mr. D—— of another, while Ellis and Sammy shared the third. Naturally they fought, and Sammy's irresistible shrieks of shrill laughter broke out suddenly at all hours. At length the result, long since expected, fairly took place. In a wild struggle of Sammy's to sit upon Ellis's head—an attempt resisted with silent vehemence —the hammock suddenly split, and both came down.

The following morning we went to call on the cura of the town, whom, with some difficulty, we found in a filthy mud hut, unprovided with windows: we preferred to talk outside. The priest was a young man, broad and fleshy, of that coarse type common in Southern Europe. His dark face expressed suspicion and shyness, and covered dislike, while he affected not to understand our wants. Decidedly I do not think highly of the Nicaraguan intellect; it has, indeed, that subtilty and quickness always seen among mixed breeds, but intelligence it has not. Nevertheless, I cannot believe that the priests are such utter fools as they took pains to appear in our sight. While giving the Juigalpa cura credit for the very grossest ignorance, he must at least have known that there had been Indians in the country before the conquest; the more especially as his hair betrayed him to be three parts Indian himself. Considering that every peasant dreams of treasure buried beneath the great mountain cairns, one might have anticipated that their confessor would know something about these things. But no! His bishop had given no instructions how to deal with heretics asking for "piedras antiguas," and, for aught he knew, the great Pope himself had forbidden the faithful to answer. Valgame Dios! Perhaps these he-mules wished to practise forbidden arts in the graves of the old magicians. May be they would raise the devil himself, to ruin the beauty and prosperity of Juigalpa, of which heretics were so madly jealous. No! he knew nothing, he said; nobody there studied such subjects. The town was very poor,—with a smile and a proud glance at the wretched plaza,— the caballeros could see that a man must work hard to support his family and the reputation of his native place. He had no time to look for such things, if they existed. So we uttered a vow, repeated a thousand times afterwards, never again to ask anything from a "Greaser," and came away, much puzzled how to proceed.

By the way, I should mention that this specimen of ultramontane stupidity wore trousers of pea-green chintz, and two or three strings of little glass beads round his neck, like a savage. While we conversed he drew figures with a mule-whip, and the moment we left he gathered up his long gown most funnily round the waist— showing the broadest pair of pea-green trousers a young priest could wish to have—tied it fast, and thus girt, strutted down the plaza and round a corner. He was probably going to consult some fellow-idiot about his future proceedings.

Fortunately, Gulielmo, our sub-mozo, had an acquaintance with the alcalde, or mayor, dating from the time when they were comrades in the filibuster war, and he sent Sammy to say that his friend knew all about the "Caribs" and their remains. Accordingly we sent for the official, gave him a broken chair, a glass of brandy, a cigar, and prepared the attack. He told us there was an idol in the garden of an old Indian, about two leagues from the town, and until we had seen that he would give us no more. Early next morning we set forth, first descending a steep gully, then across a river, until we reached the savannah. The ground was for the most part level, covered with long grass, and broken up by streams overshadowed with trees. Solitary cliffs of red granite, covered with flowering shrubs, rose perpendicularly from the soil, looking like islands in a smooth sea of green. After about nine miles, we reached a poor hut, from which, as usual, fifty lean dogs rushed to the attack. Riding into the "corral," we found an aged Indian woman, grinding tortillas in light and easy costume. All about the roof of her cage-like cookhouse were little green paroquets, which fluttered and chirped in their quick, pretty way, at sight of us, and disappeared among the sticks. The old woman also fluttered and chirped in a manner not nearly so pretty, while hastily arranging her costume, during which propriety we sat on our mules, and stared hard at the ripe grenadillas growing against the house wall. Our reflections took the shape of "garrapata" pie.* Presently an old Indian, dressed as imperfectly as his wife, came and stared at us,—a politeness which we construed as an invitation to dismount; and we did so with much courtesy. Silently he led the way into a sort of porch hung round with hollow logs crammed with bees and honey. We at once stated the object of our visit, and he rose, muttering something about being very ill, and took us into his garden, at the further end of which was a stone figure, thirty-seven inches in height by thirteen in diameter. It apparently represented a woman of benevolent expression, but

---

* Honour to whom honour is due! Captain Bedford Pim first gave that most appropriate name to the noble grenadilla pie.

the features were so broken as scarcely to be distinguishable; the left corner of the mouth was strangely drawn up, so as to leave a deep round hole between the lips. On the head was a very rude turban of some kind, which apparently hung down the back behind the ears. The arms fell straight down the sides, but from the elbow they rested across the body at right angles; the left, adorned with a bracelet, being about six inches above the right,—an arrangement simply wrought by lengthening the right humerus six inches, and then bending the forearm across the body parallel to the other. The art was exceedingly rude, and quite destitute of ornament. The legs were buried in the soil.

The hole in the left corner of the mouth puzzled us much, but our subsequent researches found several statues similarly distorted as to their features; and the conclusion to which we were led, was that such peculiarities were simply the reproduction of some deformity in the person of the deceased. I shall mention several more such cases, and, in the mean time, may observe that a hare-lip will sometimes leave a distortion precisely similar, as I myself have seen.

To our inquiries as to the original position of this figure, the Indian answered that it had come from a stone cairn at a little distance; that there was another there, but so broken as to be quite useless. His object in moving so large a mass, and replanting it in his garden, he would not tell; but we ascertained indirectly that it was done during the occupation of Juigalpa by Captain P—— and his Texan Rifles, who are said to have committed great excesses in those parts. The old Indian had, without doubt, removed it to protect his life and property from the invaders. I shall give several cases of such superstition still alive among the natives.

While I was sketching this figure, and Mr. Jebb was admiring the ingenuity of the beehives hung round the house, Sammy was conversing with the host, who told him that, some years ago, a horse had disappeared in a hole down the garden, and had never been seen since. This extraordinary story Sammy brought to us, and we thought it worth while to make inquiries. At our first question, however, the dull distrust of the Indian character showed itself, and without the loquacity of his old wife we should not have gained another syllable. She confirmed her husband's story, adding that the hole had subsequently been covered up with big stones. Upon this the old man remarked that his garden was an Indian graveyard; but when we pressed him to give reasons for so thinking, he closed his shell again, and protested he knew nothing about it. Without attaching much importance to the story, we offered him a dollar to uncover the hole, but he said it was devil's work, and then that he was too ill. To our amazement, however, the lazy Salvador volunteered to open it, and the old woman pointed out the spot. In about ten minutes, while we sat in the porch, very little interested in the matter, Sammy called out that a large jar was visible, and we hastened to the spot. About ten inches beneath the surface was the rim of a very large cinerary urn, and all hands set to work with bowie-knives to dig it out. Tools we had none at all, except a hoe, and it was soon evident that to get out such a mass would be the work of hours. Accordingly we sent back Sammy and Gulielmo for provisions, to enable us to stay the night. After four hours' labour we got the urn out almost entire. It was twenty inches in height and sixteen in diameter. The bottom was almost spherical, and the only ornament upon it was a deeply-curving rim. The sides were pierced with a hole about a quarter of an inch diameter; either, we supposed, to allow drainage, or else made in the " throwing." Unlike the other earthenware we found, this cinerary urn was certainly wheel-made.

The articles we recovered were—fifteen beads of blue chalcedony, of different sizes; a drop of pure gold, one inch long, precisely like the rattles worn by Malay girls; the unmistakable remains of burnt flesh; several shapeless bits of bone; a quantity of charcoal; and some pieces of painted pottery, which did not correspond with the outer jar in any way. We concluded that a smaller and more ornamental vase had originally lain inside the larger, and the ashes and ornaments had been placed therein.

After securing these objects, we made excavations in every direction, with such tools as we possessed, but nothing more was found except fragments of pottery, which abounded. In the evening we found ourselves enveloped in an atmosphere of wonder and awe and antiquity, strangely fascinating to the most prosaic. Wildly exciting were the hints thrown out by the old man, madly enticing the voluble whispers of his wife. That remains of the very highest interest exist in the neighbourhood of Juigalpa, is unquestionable. The colossal works, of which Mr. Squier's friend informed him, escaped our search; but the immense cairns of the dead show of what labour and combination the Indians were capable. Our host told the mozos that if we would make a satisfactory offer, he would show us the spot where lay buried the whole treasury of a great Indian princess, who formerly lived on this spot. We proposed to pay him the full value of every article we might find, and to give him the weight of all gold or silver in money; but he could not overcome the senseless distrust of the national character, and close the bargain. The old woman told us that when this ground was first cleared, some twenty years ago, stone implements of all kinds were found in every direction, especially rattles about four inches long, but that since the statue was brought down these had all disappeared.

Next morning before sunrise the Indian

saddled his horse, took his bow and arrows, and rode off, saying that when he came back he would show us the hoard. In about two hours he returned, but excused himself from the promise by stating " he had found nothing." After a hurried breakfast he started off again on foot, secretly pursued by Sammy. We saw him climb the precipitous hill at a pace most amazing for his age, and then he disappeared. Sammy reported that he walked to a large flat stone, surrounded by others in regular rows, stationed himself straight in front of it—turning round several times, as if to fix an exact position,— then looked long and hard across the valley at the opposite hill-side. After a few moments he turned round, struck the stone four blows with his machete, and descended into the valley. Sammy now took up his station in the same spot, watching the old man cautiously. Several times he saw the latter turn, as if to take his bearings ; and finally, when he had climbed the opposite side, to a cliff, almost if not exactly level with the mysterious stone, he stood still for a moment, as if to make perfectly sure of his position, and then disappeared round the rock.

This awe-inspiring account Sammy brought to us; but when the host returned, drenched with sweat and quite worn out, he still made the same answer—" he had found nothing." That he had a knowledge of some Indian remains, we had no doubt; his own first account, which he gave when gin had loosened his tongue, was most probably true, for it has been his boast since youth, as we ascertained; but all our offers, and all the remonstrances of his wife and daughter, only made him more distrustful and obstinate. We felt confident that his absences had been to consult some omen, or to perform some old-world ceremony, the result of which forbade disclosure.

At least, however, we were resolved to see that awful stone surrounded by rows of others, which seemed to be a landmark in visiting the treasure, and accordingly we toiled up the hill under the guidance of Sammy. True enough, the rocks had an uncanny look. They were arranged over the hill-top in circles and squares and diamonds, and all sorts of regular shapes, but around the big central stone they branched forth in straight rays, to a large circumference of equal segments. Certainly no accident had so placed any of the figures, but the central one was the most perfect; all the stones on the hill-side had been brought up to the top. Standing in the centre, with our backs to the large rock, we could see a grey cliff precisely opposite, and on the same level with ourselves. A few yards to the right or left the trees by the water-course in the ravine hindered this view. That was the cliff by which the old man had last stood, and to it we resolved to go. First, however, we overturned the big stone, in hopes of finding a grave beneath it, but were disappointed, and half an hour of perspiration was thus thrown away. After finally satisfying ourselves that the earth had not been disturbed there, we proceeded into the valley and up the bare hill-side. Ah! but it was hot, that climb! Turning from time to time, as the old man had done, to take our bearings, we struggled up until reaching the zone of shrubs and rocks, where the work became easier. Presently we gained the foot of the cliff, which also had an uncanny look. Round about it we wandered, but no foot-tracks were visible, and all trace of the old man's course was lost. After half an hour's search the heat became unbearable, and we hurried down the hill, with a comfortable reflection that, after all, the Indians were not such fools as to leave their treasure where the first seeker could find it.

All arts of persuasion and bribery and threats being thrown away upon the unimpressible superstition of our host, we reluctantly gave over the attempt, and rode back to Juigalpa. When he heard of our return, the alcalde came in, and began telling all sorts of wonders. He described an Indian house at the top of a neighbouring hill, "having many large stone chambers, paved with square flags;" of a tribe of "Indios bravos," or unconquered Indians, inhabiting a district only twelve leagues from Juigalpa, the capital of which was a large town called Muros; of their wealth in gold and jewels, their strange customs, and fierce habits; how they spoke English, and preserved a traditional love for their old friends the buccaneers. Wherever one goes in Central America these stories of unconquered tribes,—perfectly true, by the way,—pursue one. The descendants of the

Spaniards, after the lapse of three centuries, are still but squatters in the land; round them on every side are the sons of the old races, preserving a proud hostility. We made liberal offers to the alcalde to guide us among these Muros Indians, whom he said he had visited as a boy; but he held up his silver-bound stick of office, and said *that* kept him chained to the town. Sammy, who was assisting in the dialogue, asked why he did not give up the duties which he professed to dislike; but his answer was that he had already offered the government one hundred dollars to be relieved from the twenty days which his year had still to run, but had been refused. Our funny little Jamaica boy translated this by saying that the alcalde had offered one hundred dollars to the government for twenty days' rest *for his stick*, which was tired of the year's exertions.

The following day we went to see a number of " painted monkeys," as idols are always called by the natives, information of which had reached us through the alcalde. Two leagues over the mountain brought us to the spot, a small burnt savannah surrounded by open forest. The first figure we found was a veritable idol, four feet eight inches high by one foot four inches in diameter; the pedestal and the lower part of the legs had been removed, to build in the walls of a neighbouring house. The head was also gone, but on searching near, we found it in the grass.

The sculpture of this figure was immensely superior to that first found, which belonged to the class we recognize as "portraits." The head was bound with an ornamental coronet, elaborately carved and graceful. Whatever it may have represented, a rough and careless idea of it might be obtained by a circlet of oyster-shells, placed so that each slightly overlapped the other. In the centre was a complete circle. The back of the head was deeply sculptured in saltires and horizontal lines. Under the diadem was apparently a cap of soft folds. The ears were represented in a "conventional" manner, or else the entangled circles were meant to portray earrings. The eyes were large, prominent, and deeply sculptured as to the pupil, an art which gave an aspect of indescribable wrath and malignity to the countenance. The nose was gone, as was the under jaw, but from the appearance of the fracture, the mouth would seem to have been unnaturally distended, possibly to receive the heart of a victim. The arms were rounded, and not very badly drawn, the position being the same as in the first figure, with the humerus of the left prolonged six inches. The thighs were placed in an impossible circle round the body, and profusely covered with carving, especially at the back. On the left shoulder was a cross by itself. A cincture of rich carving encircled the waist, and the lower part of the figure was covered with deep transverse markings. Some fifty yards off lay a fragment of sculptured stone, which may possibly have been part of its pedestal; the style of ornament was odd, but not inelegant.

On entering the forest we found it a perfect graveyard. The cairns extended over a space of two acres; but all the statues which had formerly adorned them were overthrown or buried. Most had been pounded to pieces by the zeal of converting padres, but almost every step we took was upon a sculptured fragment The most noticeable was a gigantic monolith, of which we uncovered twelve feet six inches, and how much more there may have been we could not tell. If this figure was mounted on a pedestal, it must have been colossal indeed. The head was much battered, but we could make out no trace of the features—from what remained, it would almost seem as if it had never represented anything human. A great ridge of stone, squarely cut, covered the place where the mouth should have been ; and a circle like an immense eye was in the centre of the forehead. On the breast was a figure of two triangles placed point to point, and beneath that were the breasts. On the stomach was a carefully-carved cross. The arms and legs were arranged in a manner we never saw exemplified elsewhere, being doubled back so that the hands alone rested on the stomach ; the shoulder blades were carefully delineated.

Next we found the fragment of a pedestal or column, the capital of which was adorned with all the emblems of Christianity, the circle, cross, and double triangle. The front was sculptured in diamonds.

The fifth figure was a "portrait," of which the crown of the head was lost. The eyes were

NICARAGUAN SCULPTURE.

closed (as is usual in "portrait" statues), the nose round and rather short, the mouth well-drawn and half open. In the ears were heavy rings, and over the right eye an unmistakable wen. This figure was well preserved down to the breast; head thirteen inches high. The face was generally amiable and life-like.

The sixth figure was badly broken, but all round the face were thick rolls of stone, evidently intended to represent beard and whiskers—appendages not more impossible among the American Indians than in the East, though equally rare. The eyes were closed.

Ths other fragments we found were too much mutilated to be of value. One, without a head, had the arms curiously bent, the right being raised easily, as if to the chin, the left apparently supporting it at the elbow. None of these figures had any sign of sex—an omission we afterwards found to be confined to the Chontales statues.

The guide told us that behind his cottage was a "monkey" engraven upon a rock, and also a "mountain of earthenware." The distance was too great to venture upon that afternoon, and we reserved these antiquities for examination on our return.* At a hut on the savannah a man offered to show us some "painted figures" on a neighbouring hill, and thither we proceeded. He led us to a vast cairn of rock, on which were several fragments of sculpture, and four deep holes, from which statues had been removed to strengthen the foundation of cottages. In the deepest of these excavations we dug for some time, unearthing immense quantities of broken crocks, but nothing perfect. The great thickness of the graves would, we knew, prevent us from reaching the body without days of labour; but the cottagers assured us they sometimes found entire vessels near the surface. We had not such fortune, and before sunset returned to Juigalpa, well satisfied with the day's exertions.

It will be noticed that the only figure to which our theory would give the name of "idol" was found in the open savannah, directly in front of the graves. Nine out of ten among the statues found in Chontales, to all of which the name "idol" has been applied, have a

* Owing to our critical bill of health on returning, we were unable to delay our journey for this purpose.

simple human air about their features, however irregularly modelled, which we cannot believe the artist would have given to a countenance intended to strike awe or terror among beholders. Some of them, as I have shown above, possess little peculiarities and distortions, which give the impression that the artist designed to represent some object before him at the moment. Another noticeable fact is that such figures invariably have the eyes closed. That the Indian sculptors could, if they wished, produce an expression of intense ferocity, abundance of examples will show. In such cases, which we recognize as true idols, they opened wide the eyes, projected the eyebrows so as to cast deep shadows, threw the pupil into high relief, and distended the mouth: some of those statues, sketched by Mr. Jebb, in Ometepec and Zapatero, give a high impression of native skill in embodying stilly horror or terrific energy. Such as these are *never* found on graves, though frequently at a little distance.

The argument suggested to us by these observations is simple. On the one side are numerous figures of human, and generally amiable air, which are invariably found upon the great cairns beneath which the dead lie buried; on the other are figures, comparatively few in number, evidently designed to overawe or terrify, which are never discovered upon graves, but often in their neighbourhood. Is it not a justifiable theory, that the former are representations of the dead, and the latter ideal embodiments of supernatural beings? So at least it seemed to us, and every discovery we made tended to strengthen this impression.

In the old prehistoric days, about which we guess so blindly, the scene on this brown savannah must have been not a little striking. Then, as now, the blue mountains walled it round—the light beat as fiercely upon it—the jicara trees still grew in line across it. But every hill-top within sight was then crowned with its stately cairn, on which the statues of the dead stood up against the sky. Where the twisted brushwood now springs from their ruins, rose square-built pyramids of solid stone; in place of green leaves and hoary stems, were range on range of statue and column, preserving the memory of buried chiefs. In front, the

awful figures of the gods stood high upon their
pedestals, and round them were the blood-spat-
tered teocalles, where the priests held weirdly
converse. How that multitude of statues must
have gleamed at midnight under the ivory
moonbeams! How the wind must have rustled
and moaned there, until the young cacique, im-
prisoned in the temple, could dream he held
converse with his fathers! Daybreak in that
lonely savannah is even yet a glorious sight;
but fancy it in old days, when the first ray
above the mountain tops sparkled upon a crowd
of worshippers; when a hundred painted banners fluttered in the keen fresh light, as the
pipes wailed out their morning hymn, and the
deer-hide cymbals clanged. The sun mounts up,
and the people circle round in the sacred dance;
the priests chant from the teocalle, sprinkling
blood to the five gods. Slowly the long-hid
cacique comes forth from the temple door, and
climbs into his gold-spread litter. Then the
procession streams back over the hills, the people turning as they go to look once more upon
that stately scene; and in the night comes the
Spaniard, to crush them down into a barbarism

more hopeless than that from which they had so lately risen. Ah! To have seen, but for a moment, that brightness of the earth, which faded out with the savage old world! We might have been happier, some of us, had we lived in those barbarous days, when men loved and trusted, and thought they knew.

I regret to relate that we had a serious difficulty with the alcalde on our return to Juigalpa; he accused me of calling him a liar, in speaking to Mr. Jebb. Anything more utterly ridiculous could not be conceived, for, independently of the fact that his stories had proved true in every case in which we had investigated them, there was not a soul within thirty miles who could speak or understand one word of English, and we pointed out to him the absurdity of supposing that I should talk to Mr. Jebb in Spanish. But his stolid Indian obstinacy was immovable either to reason or kindness. In vain we showed him that the guide, from whom he had the charge, could not even repeat the English word I had used, nor professed to understand that language. In vain I made a formal denial, and sent off to seek the man, who had prudently left the town. He sat stolid and silent; returning to the charge with a provoking obstinacy which finally overcame our patience, and we turned him out of the house with a present for his previous services.

The difficulty had no doubt risen from the tale he told us of an Indian "house of stone" on a neighbouring mountain. This had excited the indignation of our host—who asserted it to be a natural cavern of considerable extent—which we found to be the truth. It is but just to the alcalde, who may be of more service to future travellers than to us, to observe that he mentioned this antiquity as a story which had been told to him.

The following day we rode out to this "house of stone," which we failed to find. Several caverns were discovered, but the distance was too great to allow a careful examination of them; besides that, the candles had been forgotten, and, as a rule, one prefers light for a free tiger-fight.

Next day we left for Libertad, the great mining centre, which lies about thirty-five miles from Juigalpa. Unfortunately the bolting of a mule caused delay in starting, and eleven o'clock struck from the crazy mud campanile before we fairly set out. Our road was mountainous in the extreme; more than two hours were spent in climbing the lofty chain which looks down on Juigalpa, but on gaining the summit there was a view below us such as few have ever seen. Mountains on mountains, craters and lakes, hills and savannahs, winding rivers, dark lines of forest, and green patches of cultivation—what a scene of lovely chaos it was! In the midst, far below us, were the grey roofs of Juigalpa, and far, far below again, was the level of the lake, sparkling palely against the horizon.

Upward still we went—over burnt-up grass land and smooth volcanic hills, through dried and stony water-beds, over tracts of blinding sand—until the afternoon was far advanced. No wonder travellers have talked of Indian fortresses and massive earthworks in this region; the round grey hills covered with fine grass, the soft shapes of natural rocks, the piling of great boulders one above another in strange conjunction, might well lead them into error. But

Nature is a greater architect than the best of us; her chance work in this wild region is more lasting than man could raise.

Nothing remarkable happened during the morning; we forded a broad river, and most of us got wet; Mr. D—— was thrown from his horse six times; we killed two snakes, and I had an awful combat with a wounded macaw. About three o'clock rain began heavily; the clouds settled down on the mountain tops, wrapping us round in their chilly curls. Miserably we rode onwards, slipping and stumbling on the clayey soil, until suddenly we beheld a phenomenon rarely met with in Chontales—we beheld a house. This noble structure was situate on the further side of a very deep ravine, clothed, covered, choked, with tall bamboos. No opening the size of a hand could be seen in the tender foliage, which looked like a sea of lace; it was a lovely sight even in that shivering storm. Sammy and Gulielmo were sent forward to ask the way, while we halted halfway down the precipitous cliff. A message was returned that Libertad was not an half-hour's ride further, and the road was straight on.

Would any being on this earth but a "Greaser" have told such a lie in such a case? Libertad was fifteen long miles off, and with deluged roads and swollen streams, a night march might have cost us our lives. But the message answered its purpose. We rode cheerily on down the precipice, and the churlish squatter had no "he-mules" * in his house that night.

At the end of an hour we could see nothing of Libertad, and Gulielmo, recognizing the locality, declared we were still three mountain leagues distant. As far as the eye could reach the savannah was flat as the sea, except for one small copse before us. We were riding by the edge of a swamp luxuriant in white lilies and cane-bamboos, which looked soft and glossy as green silk in that driving rain. Darkness began to set in. The wind shrieked strangely over that naked table-land, gathering the rain before it, and dashing a sheet of water in our faces. To go on was most dangerous, if not impossible, but what a place to camp! The strong sword-grass round was half as high as ourselves; the ground was a puddle; in such a deluge the

* "Machos." So foreigners are kindly called by the "Greasers."

fire would never burn; the wind was rising to storm pitch. But we could not keep our seats in the saddle, we *must* camp—and camp we did, under shelter of the thicket.

Such a night it was—such a night! We found two or three big stones by a stream, and carried them up for seats. To lie down was impossible. Our fire was scattered and whirled about, and half-quenched by the rain; every stick was sopped with wet. How the wind howled and yelled over the mountain, and drove the stinging rain in sheets before it! Closer and closer we crouched together, shivering under our rugs. Quicker and quicker came the blasts, fiercer the yells, more unearthly the moanings from the bamboo swamp. Such a night!

Of course Gulielmo did Mark Tapley in style. He sang songs; he told stories; he hummed fandangos; he chaffed his fellow mozo; he tickled Sammy until both screamed out. We also did our best to keep things alive; we also sang songs, and made jokes; but the sounds of the tempest were too ghastly for northern spirits to bear, and soon we found ourselves in the discussion of those ghost-stories which all men delight to hear. Suddenly, in the midst of an awful occurrence which took place in Mr. Jebb's family shortly before the memory of man, Salvador gave vent to a breathless hiss, commanding attention. The silence was deathly, except for the distant moan of the wind and the "swish" of the rain. Then a strange, low sound reached our ears. It was not a growl, nor a purr, nor a grunt, but a combination of all these. Then the yelling wind swallowed it up. At the next pause it came again from the other side. "What's that?" I said. (If my strict words were, " What the devil's that?" surely something may be allowed to the strangeness of our situation.) " Dos leones, señor!" muttered Salvador, while Gulielmo quietly drew his machete.

This much increased the interest of the position. To be interrupted in a ghost-story of thrilling horror by the tender caterwauling of two pumas, is a sensation that has necessarily been felt by very few; but when to this excitement is added that of sitting on a mountain top, wet through, with a wind singing round like a very chorus of devils, it will, I think, be yielded that our position had striking novelty and considerable dramatic value. "Where are the mules?" asked Mr. Jebb. "They are all right," said Gulielmo. "The lions won't attack *them*." "Bless me!" we thought. "Are they likely to attack *us?*" So we got our rifles ready.*

But the lions did not seem to stir from their place at the further side of the thicket, though at intervals they showed their watchfulness by uttering that strange cry. In spite of our efforts to keep awake, we gradually dozed off, leaning one against the other. I may have thus slept brokenly for an hour, when, on a sudden, that weird consciousness of something unknown and dangerous, which most people have felt once or twice by the midnight camp-fire, awoke me.† My head was resting on Mr. Jebb's shoulder, and I felt that he also was awake and listening.

---

* Of course this was a grim joke of Gulielmo's, unless he thought we were near the lions' den, in which case they might *possibly* attack us; a chance which of course we saw as well as he. The mules were not tethered, and consequently safe.

† No one can have less belief in presentiments and so on than I, but I have felt this strange warning too often to be deceived. I never knew a man to wake with such a feeling when there was not some pressing danger near, either of wild beasts or of wild men. The puma is the most dangerous animal at night that exists. He is too cowardly to attack in the daytime, but he never misses an opportunity in the darkness.

Quietly I grasped my revolver, and drawing it cautiously from the belt, faced round quick. Our fire had burned so low that nothing could be seen by either of us; but in the silence between two gusts we heard a rattle and scratching, as if of the claws of some heavy animal striking against loose bark. Till that moment I had not thought of the lions; but the recollection of their neighbourhood flashed through me in a moment. " He's up a tree," whispered Mr. Jebb. " Let us have a shot at him. Don't wake the others." The idea was as mad as possible ; but we sallied out into the darkness with a firm resolve to take a shot at the first living thing we saw. But on standing up, the fierce wind cut through our soaked clothing with positive pain, it was so bitter cold. Our shaking hands could scarcely hold the rifle; we were blinded with rain. After a few steps in the grey and sheeted darkness, the impossibility of success was evident; but not until both of us had tumbled into a deep-cut brook, did we give up this notable attempt to " catch a lion."

This little diversion restored cheerfulness; we

stirred up the fire, and lit the "merry pipe." Slowly the long night dragged through, with occasional glimpses of fair weather. We cared little, in our blotting-paper condition, whether it rained or cleared; but had hopes been built upon these momentary pauses, they must soon have miserably died After five minutes of calm a low moaning sound would reach our ears; quickly it grew and neared; then down upon us came the squall, with a wild yell of triumph, dashing the rain in our faces. Such a long, ghastly night!

Also we had "garrapatas" by millions. This interesting creature is known in Europe by the unassuming name of " tick "—a simple appellation, justified by the insignificance of the part he plays there; but in Nicaragua four syllables at least are required to express his dignity and importance. In size he varies from the big fellows as large as a pea, but quite flat, to the tiny little villains as small as a pin's head. We used to complain of this torment in the East, but we knew not of what we were talking. Rather should we have gone on our knees and thanked Goodness we were not, as the Nica-

raguans are, fevered, tortured, almost eaten up
by this plague. I have seen a medical work,
called "Hunt on the Skin," and in his advertisements the author mentions, with just pride, that it
has already reached its tenth thousand. I can
assure that gentleman that his work reaches its
fiftieth thousand every day in Libertad alone.
Ten steps from the door, in any direction, will necessitate the use of Hunt on returning; for the
horrid little garrapatas cling to the shrubs, the
weeds, the grassblades, and fix themselves upon
the passer-by. After two minutes' inconsiderate
walking through a thicket, we have had our
trousers so covered with the smaller species, that
they seemed as if a handful of meal had been
thrown upon them; and each tick was already
half-buried in the stuff, or hurrying, with all the
speed of his—Mr. Westwood knows how many—
legs, to find a suitable opening. Fortunately it
was the large species which haunted our camp
that memorable night, and the tickling of their
movements generally betrayed them before commencing operations. But if their fearful proceedings be not interrupted, they will bury head and
shoulders in the flesh, kicking out their hind-

legs, meanwhile, in a manner awful to behold. When too roughly extracted they are apt to leave their jaws in the skin, and an unpleasant sore results. The best mode is to touch them with a cigar, or to drop a little oil upon them. Had it been the tiny species which infested us that night, some of us might have been seriously affected by their attacks. Madame Mestayer, the wife of our host at Granada, was once driven into a fever, and a severe one too, by accidentally riding through a nest of them.

At length the dull dawn appeared; the mules were caught and saddled, and we set forth again. Mr. Jebb and I forged a long way ahead of the main party, which was detained by the bolting of Sammy's beast. The track led us over mountain tops, separated one from another by small streams flowing between banks of precipitous rock. Some of these descents were rather startling to the boldest rider; and it was fortunate we had acquired so much confidence in the sure feet of our mules as not to attempt to guide them. Had we done so, broken necks would certainly have been our portion. Conceive a bed of solid stone, inclining at an angle of forty-five degrees, slippery as ice, and trickling with the drainage of last night's rain; fancy the delight of riding sixty or seventy feet over such a road down to a rocky stream, half-hidden by long bamboos, and swollen to double its natural volume. Two or three of these pleasant bits we passed, and reached a deep, weed-grown pool, in which Mr. Jebb decided to bathe. I pushed on towards the town, and at length, about ten o'clock, came in sight of a ruined wall, surmounted by ten or twelve rotten crosses of wood—the cemetery of Libertad.

A dreary place to lie in. Crowning a hill as it does, the rains and winds that sweep the table-land play wild work with the rude wooden monuments. The gate had fallen rotting away, and roaming cattle sought shelter among the graves. Time and storms had battered at the wall until it fell before them, and rank grass and weeds waved level over the forgotten dead. As I drew near, a yellow snake crept stealthily under the stones. Verily the Indian tombs will bear the memory of their builders when the bones of the conquerors have returned unheeded to the dust.

CHAPTER IV.

The gold country of Libertad — Wandering diggers — Crowded lodgings—Mr. D——'s bed—Gold-mining—Tomb-breaking on a large scale—Corale snake—The find—The second cairn—Country round Libertad—Idols—Amusements—We give a ball—The national dance—Wonderful exhibitions of devotion—Christmas Day at the diggings—Other Christmas Days—A narrow escape—Days of excitement—Reflections upon the fine old massacre of former times—Kind warnings from the women—Another Frio story—The final challenge—Leave Libertad—A mighty bird—Cannibal fish—An alligator's walk—Colossal head—Advice to future antiquarians—A long ride—A pleasant camp—An opinion about the canal scheme.

THE first thing I saw, on descending into the deep valley which holds the town, was two natives tramping quickly through the red clay, clad, as to their legs, in long knee-boots. The sight amazed me. " Verily," I said, "here is a new country !" No one ever saw or heard of a Nicaraguan walking fast, and as to long boots— verily, a new country ! Once upon a time I was in company with an American doctor and a young caballero, who belonged to the "first families," and kept a fancy store in the plaza. The doctor told me that, being in the street some time since with this gentleman, he had requested him to walk faster, as he found it impossible to stand in his tracks at the Central American pace. Whereupon Young Nicaragua,—"Why walk quick? I have nothing to do, you know, until the café opens at night. We always go slow; it makes the time pass!" The caballero, who had been educated in England, by the way,* smiled when the story was told, with the air of a man justly conscious of having uttered a profound truth.

Inquiring for the hotel from these booted wonders, they directed me with a quickness and simplicity which completed my amazement. By following their instructions, I reached a neat little

---

* A considerable number of boys are sent from Nicaragua to be educated at Stoneyhurst, and other Roman Catholic "seminaries" in England and France. We cannot say that we noticed any particular profit they had derived from this advantage. It seems, from their own account, that these schools are so crowded with foreign boys as to have nothing English about them, except their locality. Our games were scarcely known there by name; and as to education, there was none, to judge by results.

adobe house, almost the first in the town, and halting in front of the neat little verandah, I shouted loud and long. After a while appeared Mrs. Bulay, the American hostess. She greeted me with much cordiality, but explained that illness compelled her to refuse travellers; and besides, that her rooms were let (Rooms let in Nicaragua!). No doubt, however, I could procure accommodation at the store of Messrs. Wolfe and De Baruelle,* a little below, whither I proceeded. Boots in every direction, big beards, quick paces!

The town of Libertad, though at the time of our visit it contained a smaller population than Juigalpa or Matagalpa, is the virtual capital of Chontales; and in prosperity, energy, and future importance, this hamlet surpasses Granada and Leon together. The existence of gold-bearing quartz of a very rich character in the neighbourhood has long been known; some mines, productive to this day, were worked immediately after the conquest. But the activity here soon ceased. Nicaragua was fated to bear the worst

* I am quite sure our Libertad friends will pardon me if I have spelt their names incorrectly. I have nothing to guide me except the sound, and for all mistakes I do apologise.

evils of that villanous system which barbarised the populations of Spanish America. Only four years after its discovery it was laid waste by the civil wars of the conquerors; within twenty years Hernandez de Contreras engaged this, his father's government, in his bold attempt to conquer the whole Indies; and when his death caused the failure of this amazing scheme, the vengeance of Spain was exercised upon his unhappy subjects. Next came savage cruelties upon the Indians, which sometimes roused a savage retaliation. Oviedo says that the natives so loved their beautiful lakes and fertile plains, that they preferred to die a barbarous death among them, rather than seek refuge in the mountains; and thus Nicaragua attained a pre-eminence of cruel bloodshed even in the viceroyalty of Mexico. Then came the buccaneers, who sacked its every city in turn, and reduced the rich Pacific shore to a barren wilderness. Then the English invasion, partial revolts, and at length the war of Independence, since which time Nicaragua has never known two years of tranquillity :—surely a devoted land, in which the sins of the fathers are visited again and again upon the children.

The population of Libertad was variously estimated to us from eight hundred to twelve hundred.* I should think the former above the mark, but in these scattered, irregular villages, it is difficult to form more than the roughest guess. The natives are not handsomer than in other parts of the country,—perhaps less so. Marks of negro blood—thick lips, crisp hair, and dingy hands—are more common among them than round the lakes; but mentally they are immensely superior, having benefited much by foreign presence. Their houses are of cane or adobe, as elsewhere, and their mode of life similar, except in a quickness which I have already mentioned. At that time the foreigners were about fifty in number, of whom the great majority were Frenchmen; but England, Italy, the States, Spain, and Germany were all represented, and the "Jamaica Creole" was in force. These men had mostly been wandering all their lives, and at length, without any concert or invitation, had found rest for their feet in this out-of-the-way Dorado, of

* It must be borne in mind that my statements of population, condition, and so on, are applicable to the Christmas of 1865-6. Since we left, extraordinary changes have no doubt taken place, and many more may be looked for in this wealthy region.

which we have but just heard across the Atlantic. Some had been there ten, fifteen years, some only a few months; but to our inquiry why they had come, how they had heard of such a spot, the answer was always the same. "Ah, mais je suis venu comme ça, vous savez—en voyageant." Strange histories there were among these jetsoms of Europe. One had been a peaceable "conducteur d'omnibus" in Paris for eighteen years, and then, " comme ça," had turned up in Libertad to make a comfortable fortune; another had worn the turban and the red " bags " of a zouave through many years; a third had been a pastry-cook in the old Rue de Provence; a fourth was a real Cordon Bleu, who had pocketed his thousand francs for superintending an international banquet; of sailors we had half a dozen, and every man of us was more or less a soldier. Good faith! we were a motley crew in Libertad.

There is no " gold-washing" in Nicaragua, or at least, none has yet been found; scientific mining is necessary to raise the ore. The capital required for such work, these wandering foreigners, of course, cannot boast; but, on the other hand, they have clear heads, and strong arms, and energy to spare

—points in which the owners of the mines are notably deficient. A bargain is therefore struck between the workers and the capitalists, to the advantage of both. To take as an example the San Juan mine, which is considered the surest and the richest of those yet discovered. It belongs to a lawyer, who rightly feels himself better fitted for studying the ridiculous formularies of the Civil Code, than for the life of constant vigilance and anxiety which the charge of a gold mine entails. Accordingly, he has taken as his agents two Frenchmen named Jackson (!) and put everything under their control, without the slightest risk on their part, and without requiring the advance of one sou. After all expenses are paid, these lucky fellows take two-thirds of profits, leaving the remainder to the owner, whose mine it is, and whose funds they are that work it. This arrangement has been the model for many others; and can one wonder that the foreigners take a high tone with a people which, while thus confessing its inferiority, still ventures to regard them with an insolent disdain as irritating as it is ridiculous?

Mining in Libertad seems to be very speculative work. The country has suffered such violent convulsions, and is still undergoing so much change from volcanic action, that a vein of rich ore will frequently be found broken into fragments, which must be sought without the slightest clue to their position. From day to day the owners of a mine cannot feel sure that their lode will not fly suddenly away, leaving them the pleasing alternative of abandoning the works, or of honeycombing the earth with random shafts, in hopes of recovery.* This is an additional reason why foreigners, even when they have made the capital, still prefer to work for another, rather than risk their earnings in a speculation of their own. Few of them have saved fortunes, and fewer still care to do so. After a lucky stroke they fly off to New York for a few months, and get through their "pile" royally. One Alsatian gentleman, M. Etienne, had the reputation among his comrades of possessing a good many thousand dollars, though he had several times gone through the squeezing process at New York. M. Jackson also probably found it diffi-

* The reader will understand that I am only giving a faithful report of what we heard.

cult to spend his share of the San Juan profits; the Cordon Bleu was considered a " warm man ;" but most of them were merry, reckless fellows, living so far off among the mountains, that a day's holiday in the town was an immense excitement. Libertad is not, and never can be, the big gambling field that California and Australia were ; but before we left the country there were evident signs of an approaching " rush," insignificant indeed compared with the wholesale migrations of the diggings, but sufficiently severe for an unpeopled district like Chontales. Scouts and " prospectors " were coming in from San Francisco, and English agents monopolized the limited lodgings in the village. One gentleman in Granada even went so far as to make a speculation in land, which he bought for a mere song, and long before this he has no doubt advertised " Building Lots." If Libertad should ever take its place among the city queens of the earth—and I see no reason why it should not— we can boast that we saw it at its very small beginning. By the last accounts I heard there was already a resident foreign population of three hundred hardy fellows, whose compact and perhaps aggressive influence must make itself felt in the feeble system of the republic. These men belong to a class very different from the rowdies who flocked to California from every hulk in Heathendom. As I have already stated, "gold dirt" has not hitherto been found in Nicaragua,* and any man emigrating to the mines must either work for wages, or else possess some capital; just such a class, in fact, as makes the very best colonists. Under these circumstances common sense would suggest a peculiarly soothing and careful conduct on the part of the authorities towards men—principally English and Americans now—more apt than all others to chafe under annoyance or ill-usage; but perhaps it was only to be expected that the Governor of Libertad should take a public opportunity, during the holidays of Christmas, when every foreigner was in the town, to pass upon

* That gold washings exist not very far from Greytown is well known. A character, called Indian John, was long in the habit of bringing down great quantities of dust at irregular intervals. Several attempts to track him were baffled by his cunning; but a short time ago a party of natives found him in his hut, and on his refusal to yield the secret of the "placer," murdered him with his family. It is supposed that he worked somewhere on the Rio Indio or the Frio, which is rumoured, apparently on some authority, to be immensely rich.

them the most drunken outrage possible for him to commit. This gross and almost murderous act I shall relate in my narrative, as it took place almost in our presence. The last days of our stay were much enlivened thereby.

The mode of acquiring proprietorship of a mine is as curious as anything else in this country, where certainly the laws are in general admirably designed to advance the common prosperity, if only the people could comprehend their spirit and make an effort for themselves. Should a man in wandering over the mountains, or by the river bank, discover signs of gold in any locality, he straightway buys a piece of stamped paper, value twenty cents, and on it describes the position of his claim and the particulars of its discovery. This document he sends to the Government at Managua; and if it appear that no one has made a previous application for the spot in question, he receives a grant of the land without further expense or difficulty, and the paper, endorsed by the authorities, constitutes his title-deed. But if within a certain time he have made no excavations, nor obtained gold from the locality—if it be on the surface—his claim lapses, and the land is given to a more industrious owner.

Libertad is a funny little town, laid out in rectangular blocks; the inevitable plaza, green and dirty, being out of the main road. The streets are all wide, and red, and clayey, bordered along one side with a rude, mud-paved colonnade. Mr. Wolfe's store, the most important in the town, stands by itself, having on one side a field knee-deep in swamp, and on the other an open space cleared by a recent fire. In front is a wooden building of two stories—a glory unspeakable; but the most imposing edifice of the town is a large mansion which throws out its verandah far into the street, supported on cerulean columns. In it dwells an old mulatto woman, with about two hundred girls, her servants and apprentices, all oppressively ugly. Here our light-hearted company of foreigners used to dine; washing down such luxuries as tortillas, frijoles, tasajo, pumpkins, and eggplants, with aguardiente, and Chateau Margaux, and tiste,* and chocolate. Verily, if there were

---

* Tiste is a tasteless mixture of chocolate, water, and Indian meal. It would be more agreeable to the stranger if it had more flavour.

a "Sale of Poisons Bill" in Nicaragua, every dish in that menu should be included.

Mr. Wolfe's store was full of foreigners, who had come down from the mountains to do their "Noël" in proper form. The house, which boasted only two rooms, each about twenty feet square, was already crammed with lodgers; but we were received with that ready welcome which never fails the traveller among foreign settlers.

The gentle French priest, our neighbour, lent us a tressle couch; a hide bedstead was procured from some other hospitable friend, who never claimed our thanks; and we were comfortably stowed away in the inner apartment, which already held three occupants. How many good fellows slept in the store, on counter, table, and arm-chair, I never ascertained, but their snoring was the snoring of a multitude. A billiard-table up the street was promptly secured for Mr. D——, Ellis, and Sammy, while the mozos took their ease among the "neguas" in the

---

The other eatables mentioned I have described before. Nicaragua supplies the whole world with chocola— and yet has none fit to drink.

street. Our meals were served, as I have said, at the table d'hôte of the "Blue Posts," where the frugal fare was never varied, unless our guns secured us a few "snipe," or parrot, or wild duck.

In the evening we rode to visit the San Juan mine, accompanied by a crowd of sudden friends. After fording the river, which all took together, splashing and plunging and wetting each other through, we climbed a steep hill, by a road the character of which a page of description could not realize to the English reader. It was macadamised in a simple manner, by placing big logs across it, between each of which the mules or horses put their feet. On these high lands rain is so incessant, that the red mud and the blurred sky of Libertad will abide in our memory when all else has faded away; and at that time weeks of wet had made the surface of the hill like a sponge. Sometimes the animals sank to their bellies in stiff clay in the hole between two logs, yet we reached the top without a broken leg, or even a sprained sinew among us. With pleasant incredulity we heard the assurances of our friends, that this road was rather a good one for the country; but we found afterwards that they were true enough. There *is* a path leading to the mine of Consuelo—and the only path, too,—in which, at the most favourable time of year, the traveller's mule, for hours of march, is up to her belly in mud, straining, panting, sinking; only forced on by the continual prick of the huge Spanish spur. During eight months of the year, a man takes his life in his hand when he ventures over that road; but the gold pours in by the thousand ounces, and the occasional drowning or suffocation of a mule or a native is but the sacrifice which Mammon exacts from his worshippers. Copy-book morality tells us that all gold is found in dirt; but rarely does it lie deeper than at Consuelo.

The Messrs. Jackson received us kindly, showing what little was to be seen in that holiday time, and hospitably giving us to drink from an iron pot which stood "aye ready" for the wants of visitors. Their machinery was perfectly rude, but none among the experienced men present seemed to desire better; and we observed a firm conviction among old Californians, that the so-called improvements of our quartz-crushing are really less adapted for this work than the primitive idea of four stones and a revolving cylinder. This was not mere prejudice, either; several sets of elaborate steel and iron machines are now lying idle in Chontales, having been found more wasteful than their superior activity could atone for; and one hard-working Frenchman told me that attempted improvements had ruined him; the *coup de grâce* being given by some steam-machinery imported from England. "Stampers," in especial, seemed to be out of favour. One miner, with many years of experience in the admirable works of Nevada, told me that, by careful tests in a very rich mine where these machines were used, he had proved a loss of not less than one ounce and three quarters to the ton by their employment, being thirty-five per cent. of the yield. Captain P——, also, the able manager of the Consuelo mines, was much opposed to "stampers," or indeed to any other metal machinery, in the present condition of his works. The four stones do their crushing as perfectly, if not so rapidly, as the best of our improvements, and in a country so rude, are more suitable in every way. One ounce to the ton is calculated to give a good profit in Libertad.*

On the following morning we set to work in our search for antiquities. Figures were not to be heard of; but graves were so plentiful we had only the embarrassment of choice. Every hill round was topped with a vine-bound thicket, springing, we knew, from the cairn of rough stone reverently piled above some old-world chieftain. I never yet heard any reasonable theory for the bareness of those savannah lands so common on the Western Continent. Why does the encircling forest never encroach upon them? and why do the little copses which stud the grass, as if carefully planted by man's hand, never attempt to spread beyond a certain limit? Did the Indians sow those trees in the spot they now occupy, hundreds of years ago? And if so, why do not their seeds spread in turn, if the ground have all that is necessary for their existence? These mysteries have been so often explained, that the ignorance of professors is

* The reader will understand that I merely repeat the opinions current in the mines upon these subjects. I decline to enter into any discussion with the patentee of "Stampers" upon a matter of which, from my own knowledge, I know nothing.

perfectly evident. One point, however, very noticeable in the savannahs of Chontales, apparently contains the clue, if properly sought for. Wherever a cairn is found, there the trees grow freely, pushing their roots through the mass of big stones, and waving triumphant leaves above the flat savannah. This rule is universal; trees without visible cairns are sometimes, though very rarely, seen, but a cairn without trees we never met with.

Around Libertad the tombs are in thousands, offering every possible variety of form, size, and thickness. We had determined to attack the very largest to be found, and made minute inquiries for this monster. Comparative sizes were eagerly discussed, each of our friends vaunting the antiquities of his own neighbourhood, but we eased the matter by limiting our field to a two hours' ride from Libertad. At length it was resolved to begin with a grave upon the banks of the Mico, lying about five miles from the town, and our kind friend, M. G——, undertook to find us labourers and tools.

Next day we started early, accompanied by a

troop of acquaintances, who dashed over the hills at full gallop, in a rough and tumble manner, that reminded us immensely of performances with (or without) the Brighton harriers in schoolboy days. Our men were found waiting for us at a hut, and while we halted, one of them told us he had been employed some time before in the opening of a vast cairn close by, which had been abandoned in despair after many days' labour. Our informant was the last to quit the spot. He assured us that nothing had been found, and suggested the renewal of this attempt, already carried half through, instead of seeking in a new direction. As we were close to the tomb of which he spoke, we rode thither. It was situated, as is usual, upon the top of a hill, and the stones were much displaced by the roots of creepers. Attempts to rifle it had been made in many parts, but its great thickness had wearied the excavators. All around lay fragments of statues, but the iconoclasts had been too much in earnest to leave any pieces large enough to be valuable. From the absence of ornament on what remained, and the general simplicity of sculpture, the figures would seem, as we expected, to have belonged to the portrait class. In length, the tomb reached fifty-eight yards; in breadth, forty; the stones were piled up five feet in thickness. Truly a worthy resting-place for a king of that antique world which seems so far away.

After some hesitation we decided to continue the opening of this cairn, before attacking that formerly chosen, and accordingly set the men to work. The first fall of loosened stones brought down with it a lovely little "corale" snake, in youth the most graceful of American serpents. Such a scuffling there was among the men when this delicate little beauty fell like a gleaming necklace at their feet. ' " Corale! corale! colebra, señor! Căr-r-rāj-jo!" A blow from an iron bar soon put an end to his writhings, and he was handed up for our examination at the very tip of a long machete. His slender body was encircled with alternate bands of black, white, and scarlet, the latter being raised just as are the scarlet spots of a trout in high season. He was only about twelve inches long, a baby corale, but a few months more would no doubt have given him more respectable dimensions. Even now, tiny though he were, a man's death would have been no great feat for him: except the tuboba, and the awful "colebra de sangre," the corale has no equals in venomous power. This colebra de sangre, the "blood-snake," most deadly, and, fortunately, rarest of reptiles, owes his ghastly name to the uniform crimson of his scales, and also to the horrible effect of his bite, which in ten minutes produces a sweat of blood. Half an hour is the longest time experienced doctors will allow to a strong man bitten by the "sangre," and common people assert that the sweat comes on instantaneously, and death follows in five minutes. We only saw a single specimen in Nicaragua, killed by one of our party on the Colorado, and brought on board still alive. None of the native crew would go within yards of it even after death, and I had to take the skin myself. The body was very foul.

We had commenced working in the deepest of the former excavations, at a spot nearly in the centre; being encouraged thereto by a massy shaft of pedestal which still stood in its place above the hole. After breakfast at the hut, our friends left us, save the indefatigable M. G——. Within two hours after setting to work a carved stone was found, carefully set upon its side, which after much trouble we got out. It proved to be a metlate, or stone for grinding maize, such as is still used in the country, but much superior to anything now produced. Its shape was as a flat table, standing upon three legs sculptured "à jour," and the carving upon its surface was so clear and graceful, that our friends in Libertad could not believe such delicate work to have been produced without iron tools. Then we found the rolling-pin belonging to it, a stone bar flattened on either side, which showed that the awkward manner of crushing corn, still used in Nicaragua, had been preserved from Indian times. For two hours more we persevered without success. Then the workmen found a broken leg belonging to another metlate, and a few moments showed the rim of its table. It lay due east of the first, and was also placed on its side; the size was much larger, but the design and execution of its carvings very inferior; also it was not perfect. Half an hour afterwards we came upon two pans of earthenware, about four inches in height by seven in diameter: they had been placed close together, and the settling down of the vast pile had crushed them out flat. Our most careful examination of the surrounding earth could not find any trace of contents. It is possible they had held food and water for the dead; but in all cases we could identify, the body had been burned, and it would be strange if provisions were thought requisite in such circumstances. Two similar pans, however, are always found together in Chontales' graves.

A few moments after, one of the diggers, a handsome, intelligent mestizo, called out that he saw the skull of the dead, and we began to dig carefully round it with our knives. The white object, however, was soon seen to be stone, and with infinite care we brought to light—after a burial of who knows how many years?—a marble vase, of which the bottom was still perfect. It was of the tripod form, that favourite of Indian artists, and quite barren of ornament. The sides were so irregular in thickness, that had it not been for the solid, well-cut bottom, we must have accepted the theory of

Captain P——, who pronounced it a curious petrifaction found by the Indians, or made by Nature after their suggestion, as is done at Knaresborough and other places. Its material also was a subject of much discussion among our mining friends. Some thought it quartz, others a composition, others alabaster, which last was my favourite theory. Not until we brought it to England could the point be definitely settled. Mr. C. Duppa, of the Royal Society, discountenanced us all by proving it to be a species of marble. The sides were quite smooth inside and out, and they seemed to have been polished.

The next day Mr. Jebb started for Consuelo, while I remained to prosecute the diggings; but we had no further success at the first cairn. With larger experience we should still have persevered, cutting through the layer of soft earth, in which these objects had been found, down into the rock-like clay which lay beneath; but our men, two of whom had considerable experience in tomb-breaking, assured us nothing was ever found below the level of the hill-top— a statement which we subsequently proved at least not to be always true. But at evening on the second day we gave up the attempt, awed by the colossal labour of moving such a pile of stones.

How grand men were in those barbaric times! How many thousand souls were employed in heaping up this mighty tomb, bringing the stones for miles, and burying their chieftain with the labour of a nation? A wasted toil? Perhaps so; but are our toils more fruitful? Are we happier now, in our endless struggles, our burning knowledge, than were the simple slaves who piled these rocks, and preserved the memory of their dead for ages of which they could not dream? Our wants increase to multiply our cares. To cheapen luxury we call a noble aim, and our high-priests moon out the orthodox claptrap about the savage world, until the careless voice of heresy is lost in the dull din. Yet though we should change the leopard's spots, and number the stars of heaven, shall we be nearer to that end which man was born to seek? Surely we vaunt ourselves too much. Though our age cannot slip back into the easy barbaric world, yet, if happiness be our aim, have we so much to boast of? Death is very close behind us, and with all his progress man has never changed; still he goes round upon that axis of self, on which for ever and for ever he has been turning. His back has not grown stronger, nor his mind larger; he has but magnified and magnified his burden.

Looking round for a new tomb to rifle, I discovered one, small indeed, but singularly well-built, which tempted me vastly. It was about half a mile from the former, standing upon a hill of great steepness above a rocky stream. Its length was twenty-one yards; width, thirteen yards; thickness, four and a half feet. The coping-stones around the edge were still mostly perfect, and in spite of trees growing on it, and the tug and strain of stout lianas, the regular slope of the sides was in tolerable preservation. We set the men to throw out the stones in a line towards the middle, and this was the easier from the steepness of the hill. While they worked I used to ride about the neighbourhood with Mons. G——, leaving Ellis to watch the labourers. Many were the bootless searches we undertook upon the information of stupid natives. One in especial I remember, when a lanky mestizo led Mr. Wolfe, Mons. G——, and myself, in the noon sun, over hill and valley and swamp, four times swimming the rocky Mico, in quest of a figure " hooded like a monk," which stood on an immense cairn across the savannah. The " immense cairn " we found easily enough—that is not difficult in Chontales —but as to the figure, it made no show. The pile was covered with fragments of sculpture shattered centuries ago, but there was nothing distinguishable. A gigantic tree grew from its centre, showing how many ages must have passed since the building. I also remember that in chasing a rabbit upon that occasion, we ran into a nest of "garrapatas," which nearly carried us off to their den, they were in such multitudes.

For four days we had five men from sunrise to sunset labouring at the overthrow of a small section of a small tomb. Our morning rides to work were very pleasant. Sometimes a party of lively Frenchmen accompanied us, galloping and shouting, and scaring the wild ducks; but more frequently we trotted steadily over the green hills, gun on shoulder and silence in the ranks, with one eye upon the beauties of nature and the other upon our snipe grounds. I remember every gem-dewed bush we used to pass, and every water-flower upon the shining pools. Even the big Indian dogs came to know us at last, and changed their barking into a friendly whine. Pretty our ride was not, except in the bamboo thicket by the stream, but we found plenty of pretty things along the track. There was a group of calves tied up in a morning under a mango tree, such as would have done Lady Emily Piggot's heart good to see; there were some comical fish in a brook, which pecked at the flies with the drollest red beaks; there were gigantic sandpipers, sparkling over with silver and purple, which we agreed to call "solitary snipe;" there were funny "guatuses," which stood up on their yellow hind-legs, and blinked at us from a safe distance before diving down into a ruined cairn. Flowers there were few, and butterflies were not; but we found some solace in considering the ugliness of a hairy spider, which is the terror of mule-owners in Chontales. This absurdly hideous reptile is about four inches across—not so very big in the tropics; he is covered with rough spikes of a dun colour, and

his jaws are armed with the most awful nippers
of his tribe. Like most other ugly things, this
spider has a great notion of comfort, and in
especial he affects soft lying. Turning over in
his mind the comparative merits of horsehair,
feathers, and dry grass for the lining of his bed,
he mostly decides in favour of the first; and
midnight sees him creeping over the dewy grass,
with the stealthiest strides of his long legs, in
search of an animal furnished with the soft hair
he wants. As is the case with many other
creatures that have a bad name, our Chontales
spider is not naturally malevolent. If the mule
will bear the foul scrambling of his claws, and
not shudder too rudely, he will sit quiet enough
upon her fetlocks, shearing off the long hair; but
if she express too freely her abhorrence, he seizes
the sinew in his big jaws, gives a fierce nip, and
bounds away, returning presently to secure the
spoil. Next morning the poor mule droops her
head, and eases the swollen leg. Then comes
her master, and marks the wound. Many and
wild are the "carajos" he showers upon the
intelligent reptile, while he leads the limping
animal to his house, where, if she be of little

value, he shoots her down, or if young and wellbred, ties her up in the yard, at a spot from which she will not move until the old hoof has rotted off and the new one hardened—a process taking from nine to fifteen months. Such are the consequences of expressing too strongly a just repugnance to an ugly monster.*

On the third day of our preparatory labour Mr. Jebb came back. On the fifth day we began to dig in ground perfectly clear; but when evening came we had found nothing, and began to lose hope, seeing that our chances of striking the exact spot of the burial were only one in six—five-sixths of the tomb being still untouched. The dusk was settling down and rain falling fast, when the crowbar of one of the men suddenly sank in the earth, and he called out there was a hole there. Before dark we got out another metlate, much similar to the others. This was on Christmas Eve, and we

* It is generally believed that there is no way of staying the poison of this spider if the bite be not discovered before morning; but an American gentleman told us that he had saved a valuable mule by filling the wound with sand, and then touching off some powder placed upon it. Either the sand driven into the fetlock sucked up the poison, or else it acted as a counter-irritant. In a few days the inflammation subsided, and the mule saved her hoof.

struck work for two days. On attacking the tomb again, we found another marble vase, incomparably superior to the first. It was in shape of a can mounted upon a stand, regularly and handsomely perforated, and upon each side was a carved ornament, probably used as a handle. The rim had a " Grec" round it, and the sides were sculptured over with deep arabesques. Its thickness was scarcely more than that of cardboard, but it was not so badly broken as the first.

Beyond this most interesting relic we uncovered a pile of broken crockery, which apparently had been similar in shape to the pan-like vessels found in the first cairn, and, as in that instance, we could find no trace of contents. Then we came upon a deposit of human teeth, sufficient certainly to supply four or five individuals, and the moment after a row of cinerary urns, five in number, were unearthed. They were of the usual large size, and lay in the line of the sun, east and west. All were hopelessly crushed, and from their sides had evidently fallen the teeth just found. Our hopes were now high that we might recover some bones, or, at least, some curiosities among these urns, but they proved to contain nothing except burnt flesh; that is to say, the sticky black earth, quite different from the surrounding soil, which was unquestionably the remains of an animal body. The teeth were not consumed on the pyre, either because they had been drawn out previously to the burning, or because the head was destroyed in some other manner. All these things lay at a depth of about three feet under the soil, between six and eight feet below the top of the cairn.

Idols or figures of any sort are now very rare in the Libertad district, though fragments abound in every direction. Close by us was a small cottage, to which had been carried some of the statues which adorned this cairn within living memory, but most of them were so defaced as to be valueless. One gigantic monolith, which now propped a wall with its huge bulk, had been taken from the centre of the pile, precisely above the spot where we found the marble vase already described. In fact it was this information, given by the good-natured old woman whose husband had moved the figure, which encouraged us to dig at that spot. The mouth and chin were broken; but the stern frown upon the forehead, and the line between the brows, still gave a singularly good idea of a brave old chieftain. In his hands he held a spear with a broad blade. One female figure, taken from the further end of the cairn, was also tolerably perfect;* but five or six others were quite defaced. One, very small and rude, which, the old woman told us, had not been taken from the tomb, but from the stream below, we carried off; and it is now lodged in the British Museum, with all the portable antiquities mentioned in this book.

One day we rode into the hills, and, after a long search, found a curious idol of which we had been told. It was the rudest we saw in the country; and in fact, a likeness of humanity could not easily be made with less art. The head was covered with a pointed cap, much like a lowland bonnet pulled up in the crown. The eyes were mere holes; and the brows, after forming an exact half-circle over the eyes, were

* For a more full description of these things, and thoughts about them, *vide* Chapter V.

prolonged to outline the nose. The mouth was a slit. At a neighbouring house we found the arms, which were cut in the roughest manner, without an attempt to define the hands. The back of this fragment was used to grind maize upon. Returning to the spot where the head lay, we searched under the long grass, and found several rectangular parallelograms outlined in loose stone. From certain facts mentioned hereafter, we had little doubt that this was a Carib idol, in no way connected with the massive tombs close by. The latter undoubtedly belonged to the old Chontal race.

But while these antiquarian researches were progressing, our evenings were still free, and the amusements of Libertad are not many. There was a billiard-table, it is true, and one or two fair players; but before the evening was very late, Mr. D—— and Ellis began to watch the score with touching attention — we were keeping them from their downy couch! On Sunday there was the cockpit; but, whatever be the charm of that sport to the owner of a bird, it has no great interest for bystanders; and besides, Sunday only occurs once in the week.

Of card-playing there is, or was, very little in Libertad. Men work hard for their money, and prefer to spend it in some less rapid manner; but the Yankee custom of playing dominoes for a "drink round" to the company, which the *loser* pays, has of course been introduced. The politeness of old France would surely have made the *winner* pay for his pleasure in "standing." That reproach which all nations mete to the man *qui se grise seul*, could not be fairly bestowed among any of the foreigners in Nicaragua. All standing round the bar, known or unknown, are invited to join in the festive cocktail, including the barman; but that rough pressing, so disagreeable among some Americans, is, of course, not practised. In spite of billiards, and cards, and "drinks," the evenings were slightly dull. We therefore resolved to give a ball, and stir up the population.

Our entertainment was contrived without any of that solemnity which usually ushers in such occasions. We instructed our mulatto hostess at the "Blue Posts" to lay in a store of wax candles, spiced wine, cakes, and aguardiente, and gave her general license to invite whomsoever might find favour in her eyes. We sent up our passports to the police-office, requesting permission to assemble our friends and make merry—a concession granted with many funny compliments, for which we owed the Gallic fancy of our fast friend, M. Geraud. We despatched an envoy to the Juigalpa band, which happened to be in the town, retaining their services, which were granted on terms showing how well these good Indians had studied that portion of the Bible which hints at the spoiling of the Gentiles, who, I daresay, were called "He-mules" in the freedom of a Jewish family. Then we mounted a barrel in Mr. Wolfe's store, and solemnly invited every foreigner on the country-side to assist us in the entertainment of our guests. This was all the ceremony. On the night itself it occurred to me that arrangements had not been made to secure a "hall;" but this trifle was got over by the seizure of an unfinished house, whether with or without the owner's consent, I don't know.

At eight o'clock Mr. Jebb and I strolled to the scene of action. We found that no steps had yet been built to the verandah; and how the ladies—especially the chaperones, who are a race that run to stoutness—were to climb those three and a half feet of solid air, we had no idea. The interior of our ballroom left nothing to be desired, excepting, perhaps, a little ornament. The walls were as innocent as a newborn babe; the floor was yet untiled; and doors, shutters, and ceilings, there were none; but, on the other hand, the candles were innumerable, and they dropped their wax with much punctuality. It is true they were simply held to the wall by the kindly adhesion of their own grease, but the light was equally good. Besides, the mulatto lady was in such glory behind her table, as to make further illumination useless. Her head was bound with a scarlet handkerchief, and her dress was of pink material. Upon her fat neck heaved a maidenly necklace of pink coral, and her mighty shoulders shone like brown satin above the snowy camice. The silken stockings that stretched like a net over her plump ankles were of that delicate tint which her flesh had *not*, and blue satin slippers encircled the pedestals of her feet. Santa Maria! She was glorious to see!

Presently came the musicians, a wondrous band. Such music as they discoursed has not yet been preached in Europe; but it can boast a charm of its own, and a very subtle charm too. Some of the airs played before the coming of the dancers were such as Gounod might compose in melancholy madness. The stringed instruments screamed with a pain of melody, and the flutes breathed softly through, as one would fancy they did in the low-toned wail of a Greek chorus. Such music would be enchantment to our wearied London ears, so mad it is, so sweet, and so unearthly.

About half-past eight the guests, who had been invited in our name, began to arrive. The want of steps proved to be a very trifling matter; the younger ladies were lifted by their waists, and the heavy chaperones were thrust up in some other manner. The toilettes were neat, though simple; but what ballroom on earth could show wreaths like those that crowned the heads of our belles? Such exquisite starry blossoms, white and blue and yellow, were twined in their black hair; such tender sprays of foliage; such graceful lappets of orchid!

There are faces that would madden wiser men than Aristotle, if wreathed with such delicate aureoles; but we were exposed to no danger. I must do our partners this justice—that not one among them was capable of injury to mortal man. They did not hurt at all. A glossy yellow skin will barely yield in prettiness to our lilies and roseleaves. Some black eyes I know which draw better than Rafaelle. Lithe figures are mighty disconcerting to most of us, when propriety permits the encircling arm. But other points also are needed to make the mischief serious — a pretty mouth, a clear complexion, a good nose, a small head; and these our partners had not, not even the best among them.

The band struck up an antique air consecrated to the three-time waltz danced by the ancient Britons, and just now revived. Then it gave us a polka, and then something to which we danced the Schottische; but whether it was meant for that "form" we asked not. Then the ancient British air again—but we rebelled. One does not wander tropicwards to see the worn-out manners of Europe hashed up for the fiftieth réchauffé;

and besides, the niñas did not "perform" well, while many of the men sat by helpless. Therefore, taking Messrs. Geraud and de Baruelle into our council, we ordered the orchestra to strike up the national dance, of which I cannot recollect the name. Ellis used to call it "Catch her," which was very like the sound, and singularly well fitted to the figure. As soon as the waltz was over, the violins suddenly burst into a scream more maniacal than was altogether safe, and then united with the flutes in a storm of barbarous melody, before which the Tarantella would hide its decorous head. Our staid ballroom was convulsed before the fury of those unearthly notes. The prim niñas looked at one another with a sly smile; the muchachos bounded out from dark corners in the vicinity of the bar table; the fat chaperones waggled their heads; and our hostess of the Blue Posts beat time furiously with the foot of a brandy bottle. The musicians themselves caught the wildness of their instruments; as the violins cried and screamed, they leapt up in their seats, and worked the bows with a passionate flourish; the eyes of the flute-players seemed to burst from their heads; guitar strings cracked under fevered fingers. Whirling and dancing, the gentlemen passed down the room to ask "the honour;" and the chosen beauty sprang from her bench, and almost threw herself in her partner's arms. With a band of music and a bottle of wine, you may rouse any nationality in this creation.

As to the dance itself, it appeared not a little confused. The main point was to leap between a lady and her partner, when the latter had his back turned, and thus to rob him of her; whence the name of "Catch her." This feat was not difficult, as most of the evolutions took place back to back. There was a good deal of bowing and bounding and general gymnastics; not a little of the "Hup-la!" in which Nicaragua delights; an occasional scream, no end of dust, and immense stamping. Faster and faster that demoniac music made the blood flow, louder and more breathless were the cries, and more frenzied the gymnastics. Some of the crowd outside began to crush upon the soldiers at the door; others danced frantically in the street; nearly every one of us, with or without a partner, was prancing and leaping about the room; when suddenly the flutes sank low, and with a last wild scream, the violins stopped as suddenly as they had began.

I don't know what the consequences of prolonged "revivals" may be, but in this similar case I fancy most of our partners would have fainted in two moments more. As it was, some who had been bounding like deer a minute since had to be led very slowly to their seats, and preferred to sit out the next dance or two.

The following day was Christmas Eve. In accordance with Central American customs, every family in Libertad had scraped together sufficient dollars to set out a doll-house exhibition of the Nativity; and in the evening the populace wandered from street to street, discussing the merits of each picture, and sneering at friends and enemies in proper human manner. Now if these people, being devoutest of devout, may be allowed criticism upon the various spectacles laid out for their pious entertainment, shall not we heretic mules describe in all truth and soberness the sights we saw? In the first house two or three young ladies—very ugly—were occupied in howling nasal prayers to a plaster of Paris figure set up in a corner. Had not greater glories been before us, we might have stared a little at this saint, who was nothing less than the Venus de Medici dressed in a long robe of dirty satin, adorned with spangles. Without wasting time on this curious divinity, we joined the crowd of dusky girls who were staring in mute admiration before the stage of a little fancy theatre hung with pink calico. From the ceiling, of blue silk, dangled flying Cupids and other innocent creatures, dressed in a single spangle, which hung by a thread from their waists. The stage was painted green; it was about five feet broad by four in depth, and the back was raised some three inches. On this elevation was a bed of white satin (!), in which lay a wooden doll, with dots for eyes, a dot for a nose, and a pink line for a mouth. Over this tender figure hung another doll of similarly artless appearance, whose low dress of blue silk and profuse spangles might have suggested many historical characters, if a dove of white sugar, with one wing broken, had not hovered above her head. This sweet bird had evidently been reserved from some wedding cake, for in his beak he held an orange flower, which did not seem very appropriate to the circumstances; from his neck dangled a crown of gold, the weight of which tilted up his tail in a manner not graceful. Turning a disdainful back upon this domestic scene, was an ill-looking monk of gigantic size, who seemed much interested in the aspect of the sky. Behind were angels of various sizes, one of whom had tumbled on his nose.

The foreground was occupied by numerous persons connected with one another by the tie of a common humanity; and by nothing else. Pontius Pilate, in a spangled helmet, smiled feelingly across at Herod, who was puffing with rage at the conduct of a lamb which had fallen, legs uppermost, over his feet. Goats, bears, lions, elephants, and wheelbarrows, surrounded the placid figure of Garibaldi, who towered, red shirt and all, above the scene, making the bust of Napoleon feel very small upon the other side. Judas Iscariot, followed by a select body of patients from a pauper idiot asylum, scowled darkly at the company; while the Centurion, accompanied by a faithful Zouave with a goose under his arm, prepared himself to take a header into an elaborate fountain. Other personages unknown to history were grouped around. An indelicate shepherdess, with her blue gown unnecessarily kilted, was boldly leading her tender charge into the jaws of an alligator; while a faithful poodle, newly-shaven, sat lost in admiration of two ballarinas, who pirouetted around a diminutive palm tree, with one elegant leg high raised in air. Cattle and pigs were disposed wherever room could be found for them, but, as a rule, they preferred leaning against a tree, on account of their natural infirmities. Of houses we had several, fitted with practicable windows from which looked out the owners, decked, as to their heads, in long nightcaps.

With differences of extravagance, such was the pious spectacle provided for the faithful at every house in Libertad. Of course, such things may be very proper and elevating to some folks, but to those who are not struck in that light, they are merely a subject of unconcealed laughter, which I should think was not desirable in any religion. To see women professing a Christian faith, speaking an European tongue, and living in this nineteenth century, go from one house to another, to kneel before these plaster gods, and drone out prayers to the Venus de Medici, is not more valuable to the Protestant than to the Roman Catholic. In one large store we saw a French statuette of a ballet-girl, swathed as to her legs in blue satin, set up on high among flowers and tinsel, attentively listening, it is supposed, to a crowd of worshippers beneath. In Mons. Mestayer's store at Granada is a large majolica figure of Bacchus. When we were told that men and women sometimes asked him the name of the saint it represented, in order to offer up their prayers before it, we had taken the story for an extravagant satire. After that Christmas Eve in Libertad I could credit any possible act of idiotic superstition; if these people have not already committed it, " ils en sont bien capable." The intelligent French priest, who sometimes joined us in an evening, came no more. He had been but a few months at this cure, exiled for his Gallican spirit; and no doubt the shock was so strong he did not care to face us, though we were little likely to dispute polemics with him.

When all the Nativities had been inspected, every one went to congratulate his friends, and Mr. Wolfe's store was crowded with Indian faces. Mons. G—— gave them an account of the Creation, which, though enlivened by all the extravagance that a sailor's memory could add to a Gallic imagination, was received with perfect faith by his attentive audience. Among all the Indian and mestizo girls we saw that night, one only could be called pretty.

Christmas Day dawned for us through a pouring rain. The green swamp beside the store was knee-deep in mud, and the red stream hurried through its midst like a little river. Three Christmases, I thought, spent in wandering about the earth! 1863, in the middle of the Indian Ocean; 1864, tossing and rolling ten miles from the iron cliffs of Sardinia, with two anchors out, and a cable threatening to part (a wild Christmas that was, and few with us but thought of the day with a hard tightening of the throat); and now, 1865, in a little mud-built store of Libertad, surrounded by bearded diggers with unknown histories. I inaugurated the day by borrowing a razor and shaving off

VOL. I   Q

the unwonted hair which had been growing for the last two months. This idea gained so many admirers, that Mr. Wolfe might have stuffed a pillow with the tangled twists that soon carpeted the verandah. Such an odd, lamblike change it made in many of these wild-looking fellows. I fancy much of a man's reputation depends upon the cut of his beard.

Nobody seemed to know exactly what to do until dinner-time, when all the foreigners were invited to Mrs. Bulay's, who, it was rumoured, had found some roast beef. Our breakfast at the Blue Posts was rather more noisy than usual; but though on the look-out for romantic incident, I cannot conscientiously assert that any tears were mingled with the frijoles, or any sighs washed down with the Margaux. In fact we all thought the day rather a bore, because no one knew what to do with the feelings that he hadn't got. Of course we would all have liked to be at home, whether in Alsace, or Picardy, or our own old county; but no one said so that I heard, and the man so speaking would have been silenced as a bore. After breakfast we took a pleasant trot over the miry hills, and returned in time for dinner, which was a great success, every one behaving most decorously.*

In the evening some wretched diggers found a drum, to the beat of which they endeavoured to march about the streets. We could not say which was most out of time, the music, or the marching, or the melodies they sung; but towards midnight the row ceased, for the drum was burst, their throats were raw, and their legs refused to march. Such rows, such wonderful language, we heard from the safe retreat of our bedroom! But the fights were quite harmless, and a few black eyes in the morning were the only remaining signs of the late Christmas festivity.

Next day we had the advantage of seeing a native taken to prison. He had been fighting so an officer, a sergeant, four soldiers, and his late antagonist, came to carry him off, which he seemed determined should be done in the literal meaning of the words. Encouraged by their officer, the soldiers beat him in the most cow-

* Poor Mrs. Bulay was shot a few weeks after by a rascally boy, whom the governor permitted to escape.

ardly manner with the butts of their muskets as he lay on the ground. Half a dozen foreigners were standing by their mules in the doorway of the store, and their hisses roused the officer to fury. In spite of brutal pounding the man still refused to rise, upon which the valiant caballero screamed "carajo" several times with increasing wrath, drew his gleaming blade, waved it over his head, and brought it down with a loud smack across a projecting portion of the sergeant's body as he stooped over his prisoner. The lengthened "ai-i!" of agony that followed this daring deed was drowned in one shout of laughter, which re-echoed from every house down the street as the party dragged their prisoner along.

A day or two after Christmas some of the residents gave a return ball, to which we were invited. Our ballroom was the cockpit, a circular space surrounded with stout palings, which guarded the more select company from vulgar intrusion. Waltzes and polkas alone were danced, for our host, whoever he was, seemed too dignified to order out the " Catch her." Finding the beauties uninteresting, and the entertainment to be a mingling of European monotony with Nicaraguan barbarism, I soon withdrew. The Governor of the province, a tall young man in a blue frock and brass buttons, had been standing in the circle for some little time, talking loudly. I remember noting a thickness in his speech, but certainly he was in full knowledge of what he did. About half-past ten I walked quietly down to the store and went to bed. Just as I turned in, a quick footstep sounded outside, and a hasty knock at the cura's door, which was under the same roof with ours. A few excited words reached our ears ". . . C'est impossible, mon Dieu!" . . . "Ah! quel affront sanglant, sacr-ré nom!" . . . But excited language is too usual in Nicaragua to gain much attention. I recognized Mons. Geraud's voice. In a quarter of an hour Messrs. Wolfe and De Baruelle came down the street, talking loudly, and entered the cura's house. After a few high words, which were spoken all together, they came on to the store, accompanied by Mons. Geraud. All three were pale, and looked wild with passion.

When I left the ballroom five foreigners still

remained, two Americans, Messrs. Geraud, Wolfe, and De Baruelle. For ten minutes things went on merrily, the three latter dancing, and the Americans leaning peaceably against the palings. Suddenly the Governor, who for some time had been laughing rudely, pushed forward and addressed a gross insult to Mons. Geraud; then turning instantly to the crowd outside the circle, shouted loudly, "By God, friends! What do you say? Shall we cut all these mules' throats?" With a savage cheer the murderous words were taken up; every man drew his knife or machete, and threw himself into the doorway, or strove to climb the barrier. The women screamed with fear, and hid themselves behind the benches. In an instant the palings were torn down or swarmed, and a dense throng of howling cowards poured into the ring, brandishing their machetes and hounding each other on. The foreigners threw themselves back to back in the midst of the arena, but the Americans were so drunk they could scarcely stand upright; there was not even a pocket-knife among the five.

When he saw the murderous effect of his drunken appeal, the Governor was stricken with terror. He rushed between the parties, followed by the more respectable natives, and screamed to the armed soldiers in the crowd to preserve the peace—to preserve the peace which had been broken at his own invitation! Fortunately the soldiers disliked the Libertad people almost as much as the foreigners, and they struggled to the front, flourishing their muskets. Sullenly the cowardly herd recoiled, and was forced through the entrance, growling savagely. The whole affair, so nearly ending in the murder of five among the wealthiest and most orderly settlers in Chontales, was over in four minutes.

No wonder that after such peril they were pale and furious. Messrs. Wolfe and De Baruelle had stayed a few moments, to avoid any air of fear even before two hundred armed men; but the orchestra had fled, so had their partners, and no more dancing could be organised. When we had heard the story, which was told quietly enough, it struck us that a supper was the proper mode of commemorating an event so lively. Accordingly we all set to work opening oyster-tins, drawing the beer of Britain, and wiping out the washhand-basin for a punch-bowl.

Mr. Wolfe said to me—"By the way, your revolver is handy, is it not?" "Oh, yes!" I answered. "It is always at my bed-head when not round my waist." Nothing more passed. In a few moments entered Captain Paul, for the news spread like fire, and seeing only four of us, he inquired for Mr. Wolfe. But behold! Mr. Wolfe had quietly disappeared, and with him my revolver. We armed ourselves at once, and went out in search; but he met us in the street, carrying a basket of loaves, which alone he had been seeking, by his own report. Probably that was strictly true, but at the same time it is well he did not meet the Governor or any of his party, for certainly the foreigners were in shooting mood that night.

While we were making merry at supper, several persons came in, and among them were natives whose indignation was stronger than our own. It was natural enough that the strangers should make common cause together, English, French, German, or whatever the nationality might be, for we should all have suffered that night had one blow been struck. Messrs. De Baruelle and Geraud were both willing to make oath to the precise words of the Governor, which I have literally translated.

The next day was quiet enough, though several young girls came stealthily to the store, warning us that preparations were going on for a general massacre, and advising all the foreigners to quit the town. Some of these kind-hearted creatures we had never seen before, and on none had we any claim ; it was such a pity they were not prettier, poor things ! for heroines. All the residents had received similar warning before the last ball, but they had grown so used to false alarms as to pay no attention. Half the ill-will shown by the natives arises from jealousy. If the "women of Nicaragua" had their way, every filibuster would be received not only as a brother, but as a brother-in-law, and son-in-law, and father-in-law, and in many cases would be received without any regard for law at all. In spite of the surprising fluency with which the "Greaser" speaks his own language, his chance of success with a yellow belle is but small when pitted against the tall fair "macho," whose knowledge of the Spanish is limited to its monotonous oaths. I believe it is that ever-ready revolver which dizzies the black eyes of the "muchachas." As I said before—what a pity they are not prettier!

But though we heard of awful oaths, of lists drawn up, of secret meetings, of dire conspiracies, the settlers were too well acquainted with native character to feel alarm after the fiasco of the previous night. An Indian or mestizo never attacks. He is no coward in defence of his property, or even of his rights; but the habitual indolence of tropical blood reacts upon the mind, and the exertion of going to meet the foe is too much for him—not physically, but mentally. In the battles of the filibuster war, the inexplicable affair of Santa Rosa was the only native success where they ventured to attack; but their stubborn bravery in defence brought the invasion to a fatal stand. Even among the highwaymen, only too common in Nicaragua, the same hesitation may be seen. This it is which makes the foreigner dreaded rather than feared; he gives a fatal blow while the native is making up his mind. It is an advantage which all Northern nations have by the gift of nature.

While we sat writing letters in the store, a

tall Honduran came to us and said he believed we were interested in the Rio Frio. We replied that we certainly were. He said he had been further into the Guatuso territory than any man alive, and that no bribe on earth would again induce him to tempt those devils. According to his story, of which we could obtain no good confirmation, a certain alcalde of a town near Cartajo, in Costa Rica, organized an expedition to explore the Frio district from the land side. He got together thirty volunteers, all eager of gold and careless of danger, with whom he set forth into the jungle. After seven days' march, through woods so thick that " the sky was not once seen during that time,"* footprints of Indians were marked around the camp, precisely as in the case of the San Carlos exploration. On the night of the 15th March, while the party were sleeping round the fires, a flight of arrows

* This must appear an absurd exaggeration to English readers, but there are many parts of Tropical America where it might be almost true, and nowhere more likely than in the primeval forests of the Frio. Costa Rica is celebrated for the density of its jungle, as Nicaragua for its thinness.—*Vide* Report of Com. Prevost, and Dr. Scherzer's "Central America." For Asiatic jungles, *vide* "Andaman Islanders," by Dr. Mouat. As regards the rest of this man's story, it was confirmed to us in Nicaragua but denied in Costa Rica.

came from the bush and transfixed several, including the alcalde, who was wounded by six shafts. All who*could use their limbs broke and fled; but our informant, looking back, saw two tall Indians leap out from the forest and thrust the alcalde through with spears. He said these savages, whom he saw distinctly in the firelight, were as fair as ourselves, and had brown hair like ours. How many eventually escaped he never ascertained, having hurried back immediately to Honduras, where his party had recovered power. The worst of these ill-con sidered attempts,—made by untried men, who thrust themselves recklessly into certain danger, and stupidly fly when they see it before them, —will be to give the Guatusos such ideas of their own valour, and white man's cowardice, that when the exploration is really undertaken by foreigners, much blood must be uselessly shed.

On the following night one of the Americans invited us to a ball, avowedly given to try the question once for all. It was to be the last night for all of us in Libertad, for warnings came in thickly that no distinction would be made between travellers and residents. In face of this awful announcement we persisted in lingering, for a fine old massacre is not often seen in these days of sentiment, and we did not feel justified in missing the opportunity. Of course the threats came to nothing. They frightened away all our partners except the hostess and her sisters, and they drew together a great crowd of fire-breathing "Greasers," who did nothing but growl and "gas." Our tall, black-bearded Honduran made himself especially conspicuous by reading out slips of paper, and by the stupendous vigour of his cursing. But the natives did not seem to care about executing twelve armed foreigners all at once, and now the "machos" are too many for them. There was plenty of tall talk among those who pressed round the barrier, many fierce oaths, and much hurrying of messengers; but they probably noted that some of our party were only too ready to pick a quarrel, and from Christian forbearance they behaved mildly. I saw one or two rudely jostled by brawny diggers, for the old Californians get "powerful grisly" when threatened by any man. Nearly every one of the crowd carried a long machete ; but the antique massacre suffered so severely at the birth of Colonel Colt, that she can never recover the use of her limbs.

Now, in regard to the origin of this disturbance, which might have proved fatal to so many, I offer no opinion whatever. That angry words had passed between Mons. Geraud and the Governor upon several occasions, I know by the amusing confession of the former gentleman. That a challenge had passed—Mons. Geraud still holds a high commission in the French navy —I also know; but ill blood could never excuse the conduct of the Governor. On the ground of his office, he declined a personal combat to settle the differences between them ; and within two months he used that same office to attempt a cowardly murder. For, whatever be the facts of the previous quarrel, of which of course we only heard one, most amusing, side, the report I have given of the ballroom fracas was confirmed to us by natives themselves. Surely the act of a man; even when drunk, is to avenge his own injuries, real or fancied, not to call upon a herd of ruffians. And yet that man remained Governor of Libertad so long as we stayed in Nicaragua —and, I suppose, remains so to this day.

As we stood talking with the wife of our host —we were all rather careful not to approach that barrier too closely—this hero came up to the lady, who was his relative, and requested her to introduce him. When this ceremony had been performed with much stiffness, he began to express his sentiments of profound consideration towards all foreigners—professions which every man in the country has at his fingers' ends for occasions of difficulty. We took the first opportunity to bow and leave him.

About twelve o'clock the ogres who were to have devoured us had nearly all withdrawn, so we went to supper, and stayed later than men should do who have a long ride next day. In the morning, however, we got off by half-past six, and rode to Juigalpa without any particular incident, save a momentary vision of the biggest bird I ever dreamed of. He was just disappearing behind some trees when I caught sight of him. No doubt the gigantic feather found near Acoyapa, by Dr. Frœbel, belonged to a bird of this species. He seemed to me as large as a pelican, and the stretch of his wings was only measurable by yards. Gulielmo knew nothing of such a monster.

We reached Juigalpa in the afternoon, and went down to our favourite pool to bathe. It was a beautiful reach in the mountain stream, all overhung with volcanic rocks and clambering roots, and bordered with large gravel. The inhabitants were funny little cannibal fish, which attacked the bather in thousands if he stayed motionless for an instant, but their jaws were not strong enough for anything worse than tickling. It would not a little have amazed any spectator to observe us clinging to the rocks in deep water, breathless with the laughter caused by their nibbling.* And no doubt there was a grey alligator somewhere in the still depths, watching our movements with its filmy eyes. Once on a time I saw such a monster walking from one pool to another. The drought had shallowed up his favourite haunt, and he was wandering down the channel in search of water.

* I fancy the true cannibal fish is not found north of the Panama isthmus, but there are plenty of species which will give a sharp bite at a man's body. They are all harmless, however, so far as we experienced.

With a lumbering roll of his body, caked and crackled with dry mud, with a silent waving of the crested tail, the monstrous reptile wriggled swiftly on. A clumsy leap on his fore-legs revealed the muddy pleasure of his soul; his hideous head rolled from side to side with each movement of the limbs. I think one never could behold a sight more sickening, and more terrible at the same time, than the creeping progress of this grey and colourless monster. His path was the shady channel of a mountain stream, hung over with wreaths of delicate foliage. Long since the water had dried up, and its bed was a garden of reeds, and lilies, and feathery young bamboo. He burst through those tender webs with hideous swiftness, crushing down fairy palaces of fern in his clumsy rolling crawl. We stood close to a boulder, about three feet high, which stood in this track; and though his quick eyes must have warned him we were near, there was no escape, and he went right on bravely. A turn aside would have cleared the rock, but straight he went at it. His tail flapped sharply on the stones as he sprang strongly upwards and rested his iron chin upon a ledge. Then a mighty claw was spread out; and then the fearful eyes, which always seem so like death, peered up above the stone. With a stillness of conscious power, the pillar-like arms were stretched forth clutchingly; then the jagged ridge of the back slowly arched itself above the shoulders, while the shapeless, uncoloured head was pressed down upon the rock, and the eyes stared into ours.

On the following day we went to see a "monkey" lying in a savannah about eight miles away. The body could not be found, and the head was badly broken, but its sculpture had been fine, and its size colossal. The head was very striking, and the lines of the forehead almost grand: circumference, four feet eight inches; height, one foot ten inches. In the evening we made an attempt at reconciliation with the alcalde, and I apologized profusely for words never uttered; but all was no use. He sat and leaned on the silver-twined stick, without a change in his grave Indian face, perfectly polite, but plainly determined to reveal no more wonders. Under our circumstances this made little difference, as our health-bill compelled a prompt return to Granada; but I recommend the next wanderer in Chontales to seek out this curious old fellow. I should suggest a very careful course of treatment to make him disgorge. First, a general comparison of Juigalpa with the other great cities of the world, such as London, Paris, and New York. Then a more particular examination of its advantages as against Granada; and in all cases, at all points, the palm should be given to the metropolis of Chontales. I would also advise a profuse application of "Caballero," which has a surprising effect upon all republicans. Then make a solemn declaration that "El Caballero Don Quien Sabe, Alcalde de Juigalpa," is in your opinion a man specially favoured by the saints, on account of his many virtues; and request him to witness this deed, because he will be very proud to show that he can write his name. After this, tell him in confidence that you believe him to be the very original angel of truth and wisdom, and then put the question, as if to knock him down, "Where's Muros?" If after this treatment he does not tell you of marvels compared with which Aladdin's palace was a farmyard, you will know that you have not properly carried my system through.

On the following day I bought the prettiest little chesnut mule possible, for eighty dollars "short," about 12*l*. 16*s*.* We had seen her in passing through before, and fallen in love with her. Later in the day I made a vigorous attempt at self-destruction—not having the fear of " the chaplain's advice " before my eyes—by taking an ounce of sel d'absinthe, in place of Epsom salts. I suffered racking pains for days, and my throat and palate bled for an hour after the dose. A French doctor subsequently said that half the quantity would probably have been fatal, but the overdose carried its own antidote. It is believed, by Philistines and others, that French remedies generally disagree with the English constitution.

We had hired a " bongo," or large boat, to take us to Granada by water. The cove in which she lay was said to be three leagues

* The Nicaraguan dollar has only eighty American cents. In any case it is a mere figure of speech, as Guatemala and Costa Rica alone have mints. American dimes and French half-francs are the circulating medium, no matter how large may be the sum paid down.

from Juigalpa, and accordingly we did not set forth until twelve o'clock in the day Any idea of distance or of time is not to be expected from the most intelligent of these people, but the maps we had with us were quite as far from the truth. From Juigalpa the distance is full fifty miles, and some foreigners give a greater estimate. Under the impression that a couple of hours would land us in comfort at our camp, we rode slowly through the hot noon, and our guide made no attempt to undeceive us. But hour passed after hour; still the smooth green hills succeeded each other, and still the guide assured us that the lake was close. But two hours before sunset we told him that he belonged to a generation of asses, and commenced riding as hard as the ground would permit; road there was none at all. Darkness began to settle down, and still no "shining levels of the lake." About eight o'clock a large hacienda loomed before us, where we heard that a mile of woodland only lay between us and the boat. Our guide, who had conducted us wonderfully so far, professed himself unable to thread the forest in pitch darkness, though a mule path led through it. Taking a man from the hacienda, we arrived at the lake about nine o'clock, just as the moon rose. A free fight in the wood with a drove of belated pack-mules, had torn our clothes and bruised our ribs, but no harm was done. In three minutes the camp was pitched. The beefsteaks—a great luxury, those beefsteaks—were cleverly mangled by Mr. D——, while Ellis and I sought for sticks, under a trembling apprehension of finding snakes.

Though an European should become so used to wild life as to lose all sense of novelty in pitching his night camp; though he should come to hold damp earth as best of mattresses, and dim underwood as warmest of curtains; yet can he never, I think, quite lose a sentimental impulse on waking at midnight, and seeing the stilly moon watching him through the network of black boughs. As he stares at her up there, seeming so lonely and silent among those little stars, that surely are not of her own *cercle*, he begins to cap verses, like Jessica, all about "such a night as this." When that mood tires, he will cast a glance into the dim ebony of shadow, sparkling here and there with a moontipt leaf, or gleaming in red flashes from the fire, and straightway he will plunge into such awful perspirations of mingled memory and metaphysics, that if nature do not shortly doze him off again, he will be likely to complain of headache in the morning. And if there be any alligators là-bas, or other noxious beasts or evil memories, nothing can rouse them like a slumbering camp and a brilliant moonlight.

Our voyage among the green islands was delicious, but Mr. D—— and Ellis were very sea-sick. Mr. Jebb and I, sitting over their prostrate bodies, took much interest in a discussion whether their condition in any way added to our enjoyment. I maintained that, as lemon-juice brings out the flavour of the midnight oyster, so, in a subtle manner, the contemplation of our companions' misery heightened our perception of nature's beauties. Mr. Jebb justly observed that the flavouring matter should never be brought into undue prominence.

On the way I took an opportunity to ask the padrone, who seemed to be a shrewd man, his candid opinion about the Nicaraguan Canal. He thought the scheme might be carried through, but how were the falls of Titipapa to be surmounted? Not placing any faith in my capacity to explain the system of locks, I asked if there were no other objection. He replied that no canal could last any length of time, owing to the gradual sinking of the lake. He said the change had been very great in his own remembrance, and that the bottom was of rock, which could not be removed. What truth there may be in this report no one can yet say, but at Titipapa we heard the same rumour, and I have learned to place more faith in natives for such observations than for anything else. If Managua and Nicaragua were once a single water, joined by the broad neck of the Panaloya, this theory will acquire some additional probability. It is impossible to fix the date* at which the Titipapa became dried up. I offer no opinion, as we did not see the channel, but I think Mr. Squier talks about centuries. It is not only foreigners who wrongly believe that a link still joins the two lakes; certainly a half of the Nicaraguans have that impression. This would seem to argue

* M. Frœbel says that the earthquake of 1835 closed the channel of Titipapa, which seems very possible.

that at no distant time water still flowed over the falls, but, on the other hand, a new idea takes long to spread among these people. The thick growth of shrubs in the bed of the river will prove nothing at all in such a climate. At present the dry land between the lakes is between three and four miles, and not even in the rainy months is there any regular current, though water, from drainage, does trickle down the falls into the pond beneath. It is a question which must be carefully examined before an attempt is made to form a canal.

CHAPTER V.

ROUGH SKETCH OF NICARAGUA AT THE CONQUEST.

Arrival of Gil Gonsalez de Avila—Mexican empire in Nicaragua—Curious historical fact—The great cacique Nicaragua—Shrewd questions—Hostile chiefs—Fortune of Gonsalez—Appointment of Hernandez de Cordova to be governor—Invasion of the country by Gonsalez—Treachery—Pleasant scouting—Murder of Ch. de Olid—Murder of Hernandez—Forgery of Contreras—Murder of Valdiviesso—Amazing scheme of Ferdinand de Contreras—His death—Languages of Nicaragua—Ancient races—Civilization—Various customs—Religion—Sacrifices—Oppression of the Indians—Two opinions about these things—Where are the Chontals now?—Customs of the Woolwas at the present day—Muros—Carcas—Devincos—Glorious remains on the banks of the Mico—An appeal to antiquarians.

THE discoverer of Nicaragua appears to have been the Licentiate Espinosa, who was sent out by Don Pedro Arias, or Pedrarias, Governor of Panama, in 1519.* The honour has long been

* "Travels of the Adelantado Pascuel de Andagoya," pages 24 and 25. This valuable work is one of the volumes published by the Hakluyt Society. Andagoya was one of the officers who accompanied Pedrarias, as he calls him, from Spain, in 1514. He took

held without dispute by Gil Gonsalez de Avila, who did not set out until three years afterwards, in 1522. Espinosa, however, made no exploration of the interior, facing about on arrival in "the province of Burica," which would seem to be modern Nicoya, and returning to Panama by land, a most difficult and dangerous journey. The Buricans were a people much less advanced than the more Northern Indians, the men going naked, and the women wearing "a truss about the loins" as their only covering.

Gil Gonsalez de Avila, who had been accountant of Hispaniola, and a favourite with the powerful bishop of Burgos, set out from Panama on the 21st January, 1522, for the conquest of Nicaragua.* His force consisted of one hundred men, and four horses. Of the previous history of the country we know but little. Acosta says

---

part in several of the earliest explorations, and claims the honour of first informing the world of the existence of Peru. He does not appear to have been a man well suited for the stirring adventures of those times; but, on the other hand, he has left a valuable work upon the discoveries of others. Andagoya accompanied Espinosa on this first expedition towards, rather than to, Nicaragua.

* Herrera, "Hist. Gen." The point is of very little importance either way, but it may be noted that Andagoya does not appear to agree in this date.

(lib. 7, cap. 19) that Autzol, eighth Emperor of Mexico, annexed Guatemala to his empire; and in this expression he would probably include Nicaragua, which belonged to that captaincy. Acosta was, I suppose, Prescott's authority for the same statement; but later in his " Conquest of Mexico" the latter says distinctly that Montezuma, at least, had no jurisdiction there. Both these assertions seem probable. Nicaragua had most certainly an intimate connection with the Aztec people at one time, a connection which left deep results * upon the manners and civilization of the Indians. But neither in Guatemala nor in Nicaragua do the conquerors seem to have felt any Mexican influence in the native hostility; and, while noting the connection of habit and language which existed between these Indians and the great northern empire, the Spaniards never seem to have included them within its boundaries. When Cortez laid claim to Nicaragua, as being naturally within his viceroyalty of Mexico, neither the King of Spain nor the subordinate conquerors seem to have regarded these assertions

* So much so, that several Spanish historians assert the peoples to have been identical, contrary to all detailed evidence. *Vide infra.*

of his ambition. Guatemala, San Salvador, Honduras, Nicaragua, and Costa Rica, were soon incorporated in a separate captaincy. Chiapas, which also fell to the younger government, did undoubtedly belong to the Aztec Empire ; and it is a curious proof of the patience and obstinacy of the Indian character, that when the Act of Independence had severed these colonies from Spain, Chiapas deserted the government under which it had lain for three hundred years, to reunite itself with Mexico.

Gil Gonsalez landed in the Gulf of Nicoya, where he found a rich cacique, who gave him base gold* to the value of fourteen thousand pieces of eight, and six idols of gold, each a span long. The latter he prayed Gonsalez to take away, "as he might no longer have to do with

* All the Indians of the Main seem to have alloyed their gold with copper. The historians always give the "fineness" of the spoil. Nicoya's presents were thirteen carats fine. The Spanish histories should rather be called histories of the "Discovery of (the gold in) America," so tediously do they recount the value of their plunder. Of the Cacique Nicoya, of his people, his civilization, we know no more than I have mentioned; but we are carefully informed about the division of the plunder among these vagabonds and murderers. Peter Martyr says that the Nicaraguans made hatchets of gold alloyed with copper. Of such, Diriangen, mentioned hereafter, gave two hundred, each weighing eighteen "pensa," to Gonsalez.

them," for the pious Spaniards had commenced their operations by baptizing him, with all his people. Here the Spaniards heard of a certain great cacique called Nicaragua, dwelling some fifty leagues from thence. So famed was he for wealth and power, that the Nicoya Indians recommended Gonsalez not to run into such danger, "not knowing, poor savages, the sharpness of Spanish swords." Gonsalez straightway sent word to Nicaragua that he was marching towards him; that his desire was to be received as a friend, to instruct the Indians in the true faith, and to bring them in submission to the greatest monarch of the world. If this was refused, then let them come out and fight on the next day. Nicaragua, however, " having been informed of the actions of those men, the sharpness of their swords, and the fierceness of their horses," * sent four gentlemen of his court with the answer that, for the sake of peace, he accepted the offered friendship, and would embrace the faith " if they were anxious he should." This chief, Nicaragua, was no common man,

* This expression, " fierceness of their horses," is frequently repeated; and, from a passage in Peter Martyr, I cannot help thinking that the Spaniards trained them to fight with teeth and hoofs.

by the admission of the Spaniards themselves; and I think there is no little irony in his reply.

So the wolf and the lamb had a friendly meeting, in which the lamb gave his presents, and the wolf exchanged. Nicaragua gave gold and ornaments to the value of twenty-five thousand pieces of eight, many garments, and plumes of feathers. In return for this, Gil Gonsalez offered a linen shirt, a scarlet cap, a silk loose coat, and other toys; and the lamb is said to have been well pleased with the wolf.

Then the cacique whispered to the interpreter, Where do these men come from? Do they fly in the air, or have they fallen among us from heaven?" Then again he asked, " Whether the Christians had any knowledge of that flood that drowned the world? Whether there was to be another? Whether the earth would be turned over, or the sky would fall down? Whether, and when, and how, the sun and moon would lose their light? How big the stars were; and who held and moved them? Why the nights were dark, and why there was cold weather; for surely it would be better to feel always light and warm? Where the souls were to go, and what they were to do when parted from the bodies to them belonging, seeing they lived so short a time in them, and yet were immortal? He asked also whether the Pope ever died? Whether the great king of Spain was mortal; and why so few men coveted so much gold?" The last question is admirable in its shrewd simplicity. " No other Indian," we are told, " was found to talk to them in such manner." I fancy, if there had been many of the Nicaragua stamp, the Spaniards would scarcely have made such easy conquests.

After this conversation (and an examination of the sharp swords and the fierce horses, no doubt), Nicaragua found that he "approved" of the Christian faith, and consented that his idols should be thrown down. Then the temple was hung with fine cotton cloths, the cross was set up, and the cacique, with his family and nine thousand subjects, was duly baptized. " And so the country was converted." The Indians made two objections only to these proceedings. Firstly, being a warlike race after their manner, they protested that they could not abandon their flags, and weapons, and plumes of many feathers, to engage in digging and spinning, which belonged to women and slaves. Secondly, they could not conceive what harm there was in dancing and getting drunk, " which injured no man."

The Indian towns in this part, says Herrera, were not large, because they were very many in number, but they were good and populous. As the Spaniards marched along the roads—(where are those roads now, and where the many towns?)—great multitudes flocked out to see them, and they were kindly treated. Marching towards modern Granada, they reached the territory of Diriangen, whose name is probably still preserved in Nindiri, Dirioma, Diriamba, villages yet existing. Diriangen was a warlike cacique, who met them at the head of five hundred men, with whom were seventeen women covered with plates of gold. This force was unarmed, but they were mustered under ten colours and trumpets, after their fashion. The cacique touched Gonsalez' hand, and each of the five hundred gave him a turkey, and some of them two. The women then came forward and presented him with twenty gold plates each, fourteen carats in fineness, and each weighing eighteen pieces of eight, some more. This business being ended, Gonsalez took up his other character, and became a devout missionary. Diriangen, perceiving that the invaders came few in number, and being persuaded that he was as brave as the best of them, which is likely enough, determined to gather his forces and fight. He therefore demanded three days for consultation with his women* and priests before undertaking an engagement so serious. But on Saturday, April 17, 1522, between three and four thousand Indians, armed, after their manner, with cotton quilting, wooden swords, bows, arrows, and darts, attacked the Spaniards. But a friendly Indian had, as usual, given them warning, and they retired to the market-place, where they stood siege. The bloody superstition of the Indians, here, as in Mexico, was of service to the invaders. To kill was not the object of the natives, but rather to take

---

* Herrera, in describing the bad qualities of the Indians, says they were cruel, subtle, and much subject to their women.

prisoners for sacrifice to their gods. Seven Spaniards were so carried off, but a charge of horse recovered them all, and the Indians were defeated with great slaughter. Nevertheless, Gonsalez found it necessary to retreat from these martial districts, and to fall back upon the Christianised Nicaragua. But in passing near his town the invaders were again attacked, and continued retreating and fighting till nightfall. The rear-guard, we are told, consisted of two horsemen, four musqueteers, and thirteen cross-bow men, who sufficed to restrain a " great multitude of Indians." At sunset Nicaragua sent to treat, asserting that the attack had been made against his wish by a neighbouring cacique. If he was as powerful as he is represented to have been, this excuse does not seem very probable.

At midnight the Spaniards set out again, reaching the sea, which is only twelve miles away, by morning. Shortly afterwards Gonsalez returned to Panama, having marched two hundred and twenty-four leagues, baptized thirty-two thousand two hundred and sixty-four souls, and obtained gold to the value of one hundred and twelve thousand five hundred and twenty-four pieces of eight, and pearls to the weight of one hundred and forty-five.

By this and former expeditions Gonsalez realized a fortune, so he turned his attention to science, as is right. Accordingly, messengers were sent to the King of Spain, requesting permission to search for that will o' the wisp, a passage between the North and South Sea, Gonsalez intending to seek it in Nicaragua, which he considered as his own territory. But Pedro Arias de Avila, governor of Panama, disappointed all these projects by sending Francis Hernandez de Cordova to take possession of the newly-discovered country in despite of Gonsalez. Accordingly the new governor sailed from Panama, and landed in the territory of the great cacique, who received him kindly. Thence he proceeded inland, founding the city of Granada in 1524. The warlike cacique Diriangen probably held sway in this region, if Mr. Squier be right in locating him at Dirioma, and he was not likely to approve of the new town so close to his own seats. At least, the Indians of this part appear to have been more hostile than elsewhere; for Herrera observes that " notwithstanding their numerous defeats, it was necessary to be careful, for the country was very populous." So Cordova built a stately church and a fort, possibly—but very improbably, I think—the picturesque ruin now standing by the lake shore. He then passed through Massaya, which was large and populous, and went on towards Leon. Having with him a brigantine, of which the size is not stated, he put it together by the lake, and coasted round it, discovering the Rio San Juan, " which they could not descend, by reason of great rocks and cataracts."* This fact is curious, as it would seem to disprove the common report that the Spaniards themselves obstructed the river, in their fear of the buccaneers. Gage, however, positively asserts that vessels sailed from Spain to Granada in his time.

In the meantime Gonsalez collected men in Hispaniola, and sailed from thence to Honduras, intending to march overland to Nicaragua. Cordova, hearing that Spaniards were in his neighbourhood, and having no notion where he was, or who these strangers might be—it was in the days before maps—sent forward a certain

* Herrera, "Hist. Gen.," Dec. III. book ii. chap. 3.

Captain Soto, whom Gonsalez spied out and attacked suddenly in the third watch of the night. After mutual loss, a treaty was made, and for some days they remained in peace together, while Soto sent intelligence to Cordova, and Gonsalez drew reinforcements—from San Gil de Buenavista, I suppose. Then he treacherously attacked Soto again, overcame him, and took from his party one hundred and thirty thousand pieces of eight in alloyed gold: scouting parties made a good thing of it in those days. Cordova marched against the invaders, founding a place of retreat in the city of Leon, " which had fifteen thousand Indians in its district."

Satisfied with the gold so pleasantly acquired, Gonsalez returned to Porto Cavallos, where he found Christopher de Olid, who had rebelled against Cortes. Olid, being the stronger of the two rebels, took possession of Gonsalez and his men, treating them very gently and kindly. But one night the prisoners attacked their courteous keeper with pen-knives, and Gonsalez signalized himself by giving the mortal wound—in the back. And then the other rebels declared Olid a rebel and traitor, and beheaded his dead body in the market-place; "and so ended Christopher de Olid, one of the most renowned captains of the Indies."*

And thus the story goes on. Francis Hernandez rebelled in turn against his benefactor who had appointed him, and was beheaded, without trial, in the market-place of Leon, in the beginning of 1526. Pedro Arias, who thus chastised a rebel, was himself, at that moment, flying from the seat of his government, which had been taken from him. He did not care to wait there the inquiry which might be instituted into his acts.

In place of Gil Gonsalez, murderer, and Hernandez de Cordova, murdered, Pedrarias appointed his son-in-law, Roderigo de Contreras, governor of Nicaragua. When the royal edict forbidding Indian slaves to all the King's officials was promulgated in his province, this gentleman forged a deed of gift in favour of his wife and sons, which professed to have made his Indians over to them twelve months before the edict appeared. This creditable transaction being discovered, Contreras went to Spain *with*

* Peter Martyr, however, says he escaped, and was discovered and executed some days afterwards. The matter was of little importance to Olid, and less to us.

a great treasure to justify himself. His eldest son, Ferdinand, " being a youth of much boldness," resented his father's disgrace, and expressed himself so openly about it, that the disaffected came from all parts to gather round him. Among these was a reckless soldier of fortune named John Bermejo, or Bermudez, who conceived the amazing scheme of conquering the Indies and erecting them into an independent monarchy. This was in 1550, twenty-eight years after the conquest.

They commenced their operations by murdering Don Antonio de Valdiviesso, Bishop of Leon, who had attempted to relieve the Indians from a few of their weighty burdens. Having thus started fairly with the other conquerors, by murdering some one, they sailed for Panama, first burning all the ships in the harbour of Realejo, to prevent pursuit. Panama fell without much difficulty, and with ordinary prudence the whole Indies might have been conquered; but John Bermejo, being left in charge of the town, while Contreras marched against Nombre de Dios, was so careless in guarding it, that the inhabitants rose against him, and, after a severe engagement, defeated his force. The fate of the brothers Contreras is doubtful. A head was long preserved in Panama which was shown as that of Ferdinand, but the evidence merely identified the hat. Of the success of the scheme contemporary historians seem assured, had Panama been properly guarded.

This brief summary of the Conquest of Nicaragua may cease with the lives of its five earliest rulers. The first was a murderer, the second a murderer and rebel, the third murdered the second, the fourth was a forger, and the fifth a murderer and rebel. Verily, if the devil read history, his favourite work must be the Conquest of America.

Of the races of Nicaragua little is known, and much of our information is contradictory. Andagoya says they were Mexicans, and again (p. 33)—" The Indians were very civilised in their way of life, like those of Mexico, for they were a people who had come from that country, and they had nearly the same language." Herrera, however, asserts that five several languages were spoken in the country. Firstly the Caribisi, or Carib, which was "much used;" this was probably along the Atlantic coast, in the present kingdom of Mosquito, and southwards. Secondly, the Cholotecan, which was "the ancient and original race," and, "therefore, those that spoke this language had the estates and the cacao-nuts, which were the money of the country." This passage has puzzled every one. Mr. Squier seems to think that it means these Cholotecans or Toltecs to have been a privileged caste, which received some sort of tribute from the other races. I should rather fancy that the Toltecs inhabited the district round Leon, which is still the great seat of cacao plantation. But Herrera goes on to say that "these men are daring, cruel, and subject to their women;" which, except in the latter amiable weakness, is not the character of Leonese Indians at the present day. On the other hand, it was never thought necessary to fortify Rivas against the Indians, because of their peaceful character. The reverse is true now.*

* Andagoya confirms Herrera. He says the husbands were so much under subjection to their wives, that they were sometimes turned out of doors, and the women even struck them. The husband would go to the neighbours, and beg them to ask his wife

The third language, says Herrera, is that of the Chontals, a rude people living in the mountains. The fourth is the Orotinan; and the fifth, the Mexican. Those using the last speech had also the art of hieroglyphic writing, and used " paper books, a span broad and twelve spans in length, folding up like bellows, in which they marked down all memorable events in figures of blue, and red, and yellow. This was done by the Chorotegans, and not by all the people of Nicaragua, who also differed in their sacrifices." These Chorotegans then, were Mexicans. But Oviedo y Valdez says, " Those speaking the Chorotegan language were the aborigines of the country, and its ancient masters." Can this be a misprint for Cholotecan, a name to which it bears a suspicious resemblance? If not, and if the Chorotegans were indeed Mexicans, Andagoya must be right in his broad assertion

---

to let him come back, and not be angry with him. The wives made their husbands attend on them, and do everything—like servant boys. And yet Nicaragua and his chiefs protested against the prohibition of war, saying, that digging and spinning belonged to women and slaves. Herrera says, the men painted their arms, and spun in some districts. Here, as everywhere in these accounts, it is difficult to decide whether local customs are referred to, or general characteristics.

that the people of Nicaragua were, or had been, Aztecs. But if so, what becomes of Herrera's five languages, and who were the Cholotecans after all ? *

The Orotinan language was certainly spoken on the Gulf of Nicoya, and, probably, along the coast northward to the isthmus of Rivas,† where it was certainly broken, wholly or in part, by an Aztec-speaking race. That the great Cacique Nicaragua and his people were Mexicans is now generally admitted, principally owing to the exertions of Mr. Squier, who recovered some words from the inhabitants of Ometepec. The boundary between the Caribs and Chontals is

* Even so experienced an antiquarian as Mr. Squier loses his way in this hopeless maze. He opines that the Cholotecans were a branch or offshoot of the Chorotegans, that is, by Herrera, the ancient and aboriginal race was an offshoot of a Mexican colony. But, following Oviedo, Mr. Squier, on the next page, claims the Cholotecans themselves as Aztecs. If so, they evidently could not be a colony of Chorotegans, unless we discredit Herrera altogether.—Squier's "Nicaragua," Appendix.

† Mr. Squier would seem to think that a Mexican colony—Cholotecan, or Chorotegan, I presume—merely broke the Orotinan line round Rivas, the town of the great Cacique, Nicaragua. Mr. Squier recovered some words of their ancient language from the Indians of Subtiaba; but, while believing these to be Orotinan, he prefers to coin the name Nagrandan for them, from the old cacique of the district. Nicaraguan ethnology was surely sufficiently complicated without this addition.

not so clear. The former expression is used to this day by the Spaniards as a generic term for the Indios bravos, or unconquered Indians, wherever they may be found, and, indeed, for the antiquities which exist in any part of the country. Chontal, or Chondal, in the Aztec tongue, signified "barbarian," and districts so called are found in Mexico itself. When the Tlascaltecs made their submission to Cortes, they stated that the fault of the hostilities committed lay with the wild tribes of the mountains, the Otomies and Chontals.* Nicaraguan Chontales extended far up into San Salvador, where were also colonies, or aborigines of Aztec blood. Of the Caribs it is not necessary to speak; they probably remain to this day what they were in the times of the conquest. I would remind the reader that the term "Carib" at the present time is applied exclusively to the descendants of the people of St. Vincent transported to the Mosquito Coast by the English Government. These are now perfect negroes in every respect, except character and intelligence. The word Carib has

* Herrera, "Hist. Gen.," Dec. III. book ii.; Frœbel, Book I. chap. viii.

died out among non-Spaniards in application to any Indian tribe.

But although it be impossible to assign locality to the various customs of the ancient races, yet we have a general knowledge of the country's condition at the time of its conquest. Before speaking specially of Chontales, I will give a summary of native habits as reported by Herrera, Oviedo, Las Casas, Andagoya, and other chroniclers.

The people of this country are commended by all for their stature, the fairness of their skin, and the regularity of their features. "The women," says Andagoya, "wore mantles and another garment, which, descending from the head, covered the bosom and half the arms. The men covered their loins with very long cloths made of cotton, which they passed in many folds from the hips to the thighs. They had many beautiful women." The hair was worn in a regular chignon, the better to balance weights thereon. They shaved the forehead, and more notable warriors the whole head, leaving a scalp-lock on the crown. "The men," says Herrera, "were expected to keep the houses neat, while the women were employed in marketing and business. In the districts of Duracay and Cubiores the men painted their arms and did the spinning.

"The towns of Nicaragua were not large,* because they were many in number, but were well built, the houses of the great men differing from those of the people, whereas in common towns all houses were alike" (Herr. Hist.). Peter Martyr throws some light upon this passage by recording that the pavements of palaces and temples were raised half a man's height from the ground, while humbler dwellings were on the level (Dec. VI. cap. v.). The houses of the nobles, which were of great size, were built around the court-yard of the cacique's palace, or of the principal temple, in the centre of which was a goldsmith's house, " where they wrought and cast gold with great art." But Andagoya, who was an unprejudiced witness, twice asserts plainly that there was little gold in Nicaragua; and this testimony is, I think, confirmed by all

* Las Casas, however, asserts that Nicaragua " contained divers cities over four miles in length."—Brev. Relac., art. " Nicaragua." Las Casas had seen the country, but his testimony is not more reliable than that of any other missionary writer.

researches. There are no traces of gold-mining, as in neighbouring countries, and the washings of Segovia are not very productive.

The government was usually despotic; but the great vassals seem to have been more independent in fact than in theory. It is curious to note, however, that certain towns owned no authority of the neighbouring chiefs, but were governed by their municipality, after the manner of German and Italian free cities. In time of war these boroughs chose their own general among the bravest of their citizens; but in monarchical districts the Cacique always led his subjects to fight. It is, of course, impossible now to identify any of these free towns, but tradition claims Massaya as one : certainly, at the conquest we never hear of any Cacique ruling over it, although it is noted as "a large and populous town." Diriangen met Gonsalez somewhere in the neighbourhood,* but he is not called Cacique of Massaya. The podesta of a free town owned no authority of any one after his election.

Marriage was a very simple rite in Nicaragua.

---

* Peter Martyr, however, would place Diriangen's kingdom much more to the west.—Dec. VI. cap. iii.

The priest took the bride and bridegroom by their little fingers, led them to a small room, lighted a fire, and left them alone. When the fire had gone out, marriage was complete; but the husband had a right to protest if dissatisfied. Certain "writings" were given to the wedded pair after marriage. Whatever was the case in Europe, the celebrated "droit du Seigneur" seems to have been practised in Nicaragua. The priests also claimed this right.* Bigamy was punished with banishment, but concubinage was allowed to any extent. Adultery was treated very curiously: the offended woman was divorced, but with the right of retaining her dowry, while the adulterer was beaten with sticks by the woman's relatives. The injured husband had no part in the matter. Prostitution was legalised, as in Japan. "When maidens were old enough to marry, their parents sent them away, and thus they went through the land; and as soon as they had wherewithal to

---

* Andagoya asserts it positively of "a man whom they held as a pope, and who lived in a temple." He "had to" do this duty. Other writers allude to the droit as belonging both to the cacique and the high priest, but none speak so positively as Andagoya. The custom may probably have been local.

furnish a house, they returned to their parents and were married" (Andag.). The girl usually selected one of her former lovers to be her husband, and the rejected suitors hanged themselves without the loss of a moment. More disgraceful vices are sometimes noted.

Property was much respected; but, as in Ometepec at the present day, no man could put up his land for sale. If he wished to leave the district, his property passed to the nearest blood relative, or, in default, to the municipality. Justice was observed; and the judges were honourably distinguished by wands and fans of feathers. A thief had his head shaved, and was made over as a slave to the injured party, " until both were satisfied," a condition much sooner reached by one than by the other, probably. Such a slave might be sold or gambled away, but could not be freed without consent of the Cacique. If the aggrieved party could not conscientiously declare himself satisfied within a reasonable time, the poor slave was sacrificed to the gods.

Murder was a money transaction; but no provision was made for the case of a Cacique's injury, because "such an event could never happen." A slave's death was not punished. In war, the great endeavour was to take prisoners for sacrifice; and the Spaniards, here as elsewhere, derived immense advantage from this superstition. In regard to general plunder, each soldier kept the share earned by his own bravery, but the ransom of a prisoner was forbidden under pain of death. It would seem that each captor sacrificed his prisoner on the field, except the chiefs, who were reserved for more ceremonious execution. The Indians were bold, crafty, and determined in their continual wars, and, until their spirit was broken by merciless barbarity, they constantly rose against their oppressors. Las Casas, indeed, says they "had a mild and gentle nature," which is true, probably, of some districts; but the history of the years following the conquest shows they had considerable spirit and resolution.

The practice of confession, and of an imposition of penance found among these people, much confounded the Spaniards. One admirable custom was observed in regard to these practices. While ordinary priests were condemned to celibacy, the confessors were compelled to marry.* Secrets thus revealed were never divulged. Herrera tells a droll story, which shows how universal was confession among these Indians. One of them came to a Spanish magistrate complaining of his Cacique, who had unlawfully hidden an officer in his house, to overhear the confession of his wife, made to the midwife before delivery. The woman confessed eight lovers, and the husband was immediately fined eight times by his Cacique, who was informed of the woman's guilt by the hidden spy.† The husband complained to the magistrate, not of the treachery, nor of the disgrace, nor of his wife, "but of the sum of money he had to pay" (Her. Dec. III., Lib. vi., Cap. 3). We do not elsewhere hear of this confession to the midwife.

Throughout America, a certain ceremony, curiously like baptism, seems to have been observed. Without crediting the stories about

---

* Andagoya indeed seems to limit the confessors to one only—the same pope who had the *droit du Seigneur*. He also says nothing about penance.

† Here we see a custom opposed to the practice mentioned as if universal by Herrera himself.

redemption and original sin told of the Mexican Indians, it seems certain that at twelve months old the child was dipped in water, and mystic ceremonies were performed over it. The same practice was found in the islands, but the tales we hear are too suspicious for more particular belief.* The Nicaraguan temples were large, built of timber, and enclosing a courtyard five hundred paces long. Each noble had a private chapel, low and dark, in which he stowed away his household gods, his banners " painted with devils," and his weapons, which were very magnificent; golden breastplates, golden helmets, and " ornaments of war" are enumerated. " Large and great streets " faced these courtyards; and in the more important towns there were several such spaces, in which marketing and other business was carried on. The teocalles, or pyramids of sacrifice, were

* Mr. Prescott, though by no means credulous, seems to put faith in the stories of Sahagun and Zuazo. That the child was dipped in water, and so on, one can easily believe (Pet. Mar. Dec. III. lib. i.), but the doctrine of original sin and of regeneration, transported to America, is really too wild in faith. A prayer, imploring " the Lord to permit the holy drops to wash away the sin that was given to it before the foundation of the world, so that this child might be born anew;" or again—" Impart to us, out of thy great mercy, thy gifts, which we are not worthy to receive through our own merits, &c.," is utterly incredible.

built of unburned brick, and ascended by steps. The most important had a space on the top, capable of containing ten men; and in the midst was the "cursed stone, equalling the length and breadth of a man's stature, lying all along." The people assembled round the principal teocalle, while the king occupied a similar pyramid, from whence he could watch the scene. After proclamation by the high-priest of the number to be sacrificed, their quality, and the circumstances of the feast, the victim was stretched on his back upon the fatal stone, and, "with dismal howling," the priest compassed him about three times. Then, with a stone knife, the sacrificing flamen cut open his body at the small ribs, and tore out the heart. Then they ate the victim's flesh, and his soul went to heaven, as I think; but Torquemada opines it fled howling down to hell.

If the victim was a prisoner taken in war, the hands and feet were given to the king, the heart to the priest, the thighs to the nobility, and the rest of the body to the people, who cooked and ate the various parts in much solemnity. If a slave, his body was burnt or buried, because, says Herrera, "he might be of their own kin." The noblemen reared such victims from the earliest years, and they were petted universally until the last moment. Although indulged with every freedom, they rarely avoided their doom by the simple means allowed—that of declaring their bodies were not chaste and pure—but, on the contrary, suffered death with delight, in the thought that such a fate took them straightway to their ancestors; which impression may have been suggested by the devil, as we are told, or may not.

The heads were not eaten, but hung on trees, as in Mexico. "Each king," says Peter Martyr, "grows certain trees in a field near his abode, which he calls by the name of each country in which he is used to make war; and they hang the heads of sacrificed enemies each on the tree of his nation, as our generals and captains fasten helmets, colours, and such trophies to the walls of churches."

One small idol, of which we are not told the name, was worshipped in a different manner, but still with that eternal bloodshed. Upon this feast, which took place once a year, the idol was raised aloft upon a spear, and the priests carried it round in procession, dressed in uniforms as various as at a ritualistic service. Some wore cotton surplices hung with long fringes down to the ankle; others narrow belts; and others short coats of white linen. At the edges of the fringe little bags hung down, containing sharp knives of stone, and powder made of herbs and "coal." The laymen carried flags representing the idol they most venerated. Thus, singing, they went in procession, no man "who had legs to use" being absent. On arrival at the sacred spot, the eldest priest gave a signal, upon which all the young men rushed out from the ranks, and danced with martial cries. The earth was then strewn with carpets and flowers, "that the devil might not touch ground," and the spear planted. With this began the wilder orgies. Dancing and raving, the men took out their stone knives and cut themselves in the tongue and other parts of the body, most especially in the organs of generation. With the blood so obtained they daubed the idol's lips and beard (?), and each noble approaching gently, "with his head on his shoulder," addressed his prayers and desires to the bloodstained figure; after which the wounds were cured with the "powder made of herbs and coal," carried for that purpose.

At this procession they also blessed Indian wheat sprinkled with blood, which was distributed and eaten like "blessed bread" (Herrera, Hist. Gen. Dec. III. Cap. iv.). The Mexican origin of all these customs is evident, if, indeed, the Aztecs and Nicaraguans did not draw them alike from a common source, probably Toltec.*

In concluding this very short résumé of the general condition of Nicaragua at its conquest, I will quote the affecting appeal of the good Bishop of Chiapas on behalf of this country:—

"There is no man who can sufficiently express the fertility of this land, the charm of its climate, or the great multitude of people who did formerly inhabit it. For Nicaragua contained many cities over four miles in length ; and for the

* Very many similar customs were found in the islands, and as far south as Darien, where the Aztecs certainly never went. I think these coincidences have scarcely been sufficiently noted, but I do not dwell upon them here. Shrewd Peter Martyr, before the conquest of Nicaragua, mentions many facts, especially in Dec. III., which treats of the southern islands, that ought to be more noticed than they have been hitherto.

plenty of its fruits it was beyond compare. The people, because their country was plain and level, had not the shelter of mountains whereto they might fly, nor could they be easily forced to leave their homes, so pleasant was the country. And therefore they endured far greater misery and persecution, being, indeed, less able to bear it, as possessing a mild and gentle nature. This tyrant* vexed and tormented these poor creatures with so many and long-continued injuries, slaughters, captivities, and cruelties, that no tongue would be able to tell of them. Into this territory he sent above fifty horse, who wholly extirpated the people with the sword, sparing neither age nor sex; not for any wrong they had done, but because they sometimes came not so quickly as expected, or paid not their quota of corn. Expeditions were sent out by Contreras to explore interior countries; and of the Indians so engaged not four came back out of four thousand. They chained them up with iron chains, weighing fifty or sixty pounds; and

* Las Casas probably refers to Don Pedro Arias de Avila, who frightfully oppressed the Indians. The names of the more powerful conquerors are rarely mentioned in the "Brevissima Relacion." Las Casas passed through Nicaragua, and was an eye-witness of these things.

if by the weight of these, or by sickness, or by weariness, any fainted on the way, the Spaniards cut off their heads, throwing them beside the path, and dragging the bodies to the other side. . . . And as for the Indians, both old and young, they lived in the houses of the Spaniards, drudging day and night in a hopeless captivity. Not the smallest children were spared, nor the women with child; but burdens were imposed upon them as much as they were able to bear, and sometimes more. By such means, allowing them no houses, nor anything proper to themselves, they have destroyed them daily, yea, and do daily destroy them; so that the Spaniards here have exceeded the cruelties of Hispaniola."

Then the good bishop proceeds to tell of the slave-trade, which annually drew thirty thousand of these poor wretches to perish in the swamps of Panama, for the Indians could not live out of their own pleasant country. He estimates the number exported to be half a million; "but in former times this country was most flourishing in the whole world for the multitude of its people."

The same report is given by the other historians. Gentle Peter Martyr throws off the weight of his seventy years—"which do indeed so weigh down my strength, that, to say truth, I scarcely remember from day to day what I have written"—to make indignant protest against the horrors revealed to him by eye-witnesses. Herrera, in the calmness of his studious mind, prays Heaven that such unheard-of crime may not bring down a judgment upon Spain. The ecclesiastical reports from the New World are full of horrors. The Spanish government, helpless from corruption, is struck with consternation. "All the devils whom these wretched heathen worshipped could not have devised a cruelty which the Christians did not practise."

"And so," says Mr. Richard Eden, that worthy Englishman who recommended his countrymen to submit to Spain, "and not provoke the lion's wrath"—"and so it is apparent that the heroicall factes of the Spanniards of these dayes deserve so greate prayse, that the author of this booke (being no Spanniard) dothe woorthely extolle theyr doynge above the famous actes of Hercules and Saturninus, and such other which, for theyr glorious and vertuous enterpryzes, were accoumpted as goddes amonge men. And surely if Greate Alexander and the Romans, which have rather obteyned than deserved immortall fame amonge men for theyr bluddye victories, onely for theyr owne glory and amplifying their empire — obteyned by slaughter of innocentes, and kepte by violence, —have byn magnified for theyr doinges, how much more then shall we thinke those men woorthy just commendationes which in their mercifull warres against those naked people have so used themselves towarde them in exchannginge of benefits for victorie, that greater commoditie hath thereof ensured to the vanquished than to the victourers." And this amiable gentleman proceeds to explain that the Spaniards have taken the savages' gold, *which they did not want*, and enslaved them, which was good for their souls. If they did not want the gold, it is odd they should take such pains to get it; and as to benefiting people's souls,—it is a deal better to benefit their bodies. For downright hard swearing, and unscrupulous lying, commend me to a convert and a renegade.

Hear the other side, in its dainty old English. "So that if we shall not be ashamed to confess the truth, they seemed to live in that golden world of which old writers speak so much; wherein men lived simply and innocently without enforcement of laws, without quarrelling, judges, or libels, content only to satisfy nature, without further vexation of knowledge of things to come; yet these naked people also were tormented with ambition for the desire they have to enlarge their dominions; by reason whereof they keep war, and destroy one another. From the which plague, I suppose the golden world was not free."

"At the town of Yztepeque," says Herrera, "begins the country of the Chontals, speaking another language, and a savage people." This town is in San Salvador, and we must understand that old Chontales boasted much wider limits than at present. That this people was less advanced than the other races of the country, is asserted by all historians, and confirmed by the nature of its territory, which is cold and mountainous. But even this portion of Nicaragua must once have borne a population a hundred times more dense than it now can show; this the large and frequent cairns demonstrate conclusively. The Spaniards were early compelled to transport Indians from the plain to work their gold mines, and the proximity of the independent Caribs would doubtless tend to depopulate the land. Mr. Frœbel long since expressed his opinion that the present Woolwas of Mosquito are the descendants of old Chontals, who fled eastward before the cruelty of the Spaniards; and he boldly appended the name of Chontal to his vocabulary of the Woolwa language. In the kingdom of Mosquito there are two principal families, speaking tongues entirely distinct—the Woolwa and the Rama. The latter is the Royal language, and, almost beyond doubt, is that Caribisi which was "much used" in Nicaragua. The Woolwa are immigrants, as they themselves assert, from the west or northwest. The most important of their towns, that is, of which anything is known, lies about three leagues from Consuelo; but the Muros of which we heard at Juigalpa is no doubt a Woolwa settlement. Dr. Frœbel says—

"From the inhabitants of the village just named (Lovago) Dr. Bernhard received some information concerning the old manners of the race, in giving which they invariably identified themselves with the Indians of the table-land. At Lovago, they said, little remained of the customs of old; but with the people of the interior, the ancient manners had been left unchanged. These latter are living in a state of polygamy; but a man has never more than three wives, who in most cases occupy separate dwellings, and usually have a great number of children. When a young man wishes to marry, he kills a deer, which, with a quantity of firewood, he places before the door of the girl. If she accepts this present, the marriage takes place. When the husband dies, the wife cuts off her hair and burns the hut, and the same is done *vice versâ*. The dead are buried with all their property, and for a certain time some gruel of maize is daily placed on the grave. At certain times of the year they celebrate festivals, or perform ceremonies, at which no stranger nor any of the women or children are admitted. On these occasions they pretend to dance with their god—bailau con su Dios de ellos—as the alcalde of Acayapa expressed it. This they do, singing at the same time with a loud voice. At these feasts certain feats of gymnastics are performed, each of them jumping over the next; the jumping man at the same time deals the other a blow over the shoulders, and if the latter do not show signs of being affected by the pain, he is acknowledged as an "hombre valiente," one of the braves. Similar customs have been observed among various tribes belonging to races and countries widely different and distant from each other; they are of little interest. I would, however, not omit these particulars, as they are well calculated to convey an idea of the mental development of this people."

The above facts were confirmed to us of the inhabitants of Muros and Carcas, together with some other customs. On the arrival of a stranger the whole population retires to the forest, whence they narrowly watch his every movement. Sometimes they come back with every sign of friendship, sometimes they make a savage attack upon him. A peculiar taboo is said to be practised with their chief, but our informants did not seem to be very clear about this matter. Dancing takes place every night in the street, and one man, who had spent three months among these savages, told us that for a mile round the town of Carcas, the sound of their drums resounds night and day through the forest.

The old Chontals were certainly in a condition more civilised than this: their extensive and laborious tombs, their weapons of stone finely wrought and handsomely sculptured, their carved vases of marble,* prove it. A double-bladed battle-axe was offered us for sale in Libertad, which for beauty of workmanship and regularity of design might be compared with the best of European specimens. Their statues also of hard stone are better modelled than the more elaborate idols of Ometepec and Momotombo, and their pottery is not inferior, though different. Aztec colonies undoubtedly there were throughout Chontales, settlements of warlike

---

* In regard to these vases, Peter Martyr observes that such were found in the island of Cozumella. "One of our men wandering inland found two watering pots of alabaster, made with art."—Dec. III. lib. i. This is much the description one would give of those we unearthed in Chontales.

traders probably, such as the Mexican policy encouraged. Two-thirds of the local names are pure Aztec, but indeed this might be said of all Central America. The burial we found near Juigalpa—a name of Aztec combination—is in contrast to the usual custom of Chontales. "The Mexicans," says Acosta (Hist. Nat. lib. V. cap. viii.), "buried the dead in their gardens or in the courts of their own houses; some carried them to the places of sacrifice down in the mountains; others burned them, and afterwards buried the ashes in their temples. They were buried with all their rich apparel, their stones, and jewels. The ashes of such as were burnt they put in pots of earthenware, and with them the ornaments and earrings of the dead, however precious they might be." This description applies to the burials on Ometepec and the isthmus, and such was that spoken of in Chapter III.

Every part of Nicaragua abounds in graves and broken pottery, but the great cairns are confined to Chontales. The general resemblance of religious forms which every historian has noticed as prevailing from Mexico to Panama, is a curious ethnological fact. If indeed it be admitted that one great race, civilised above the level of its conquerors, once inhabited the whole country, this resemblance becomes to a certain extent intelligible, and the minute differences of ceremony noted between one tribe and another rather tend to simplify the problem; for it is not likely that various hordes of savages, descending upon a people comparatively refined, would accept all its superstitions without alteration. But there are many objections to this view, principally among the traditions of the people themselves. Is it possible that the Mexicans conquered Central America completely and thoroughly except the Mosquito shore? Or did the Toltecs so, imposing on the people their own religion, to which the Aztecs succeeded? This latter is the view which seems most probable. It is difficult to believe that the Mexicans at any time held these regions, not Nicaragua alone, but Costa Rica and the Talamanca country, so completely under sway as to impose the details of their religion upon them, but the Toltecs may have done so before the times of Aztec monarchy. This is indeed the vague and general tradition at the present day, and a Leonese Indian will even call himself Toltec, though he has not the remotest memory of his ancestors' glory and civilization. Aztec local names are more easily accounted for. The high respect which that enlightened despotism showed for trade, and the enterprise and bravery of the people, led the Aztec merchants, thus encouraged, to push their way into the most dangerous districts, where they established factories and intrigued with local politicians. They had a firm footing on the isthmus and the islands of Nicaragua; northwards they are again met in San Salvador; and the gold mountains of Chontales, the washings of the Mico and Indio, would certainly entice these warlike traders from either direction.

The Chontals, as has happened with other barbarians, were celebrated for the skill of their diviners. Such men dwelt apart in the mountains, attended only by two or three pupils, who charged themselves with the support of their master in return for his valuable instruction. All the historians denounce the diabolical mysteries of such men, who, gifted with more or less of skill, were found throughout America. All tell stories of their success in foretelling events, and the conclusion of the account is usually a dismissal of the diviner to those regions where his master dwells. The practice seems to have resembled that which has ever obtained in the Old World. Two days' fasting, a dose of some drug, a foaming fit of epilepsy, and then an incoherent utterance of prophecies. The business was apparently confined to a guild, and long preparation was required before the neophyte could rightly catch the inspiration. It is not so easy to prophesy as some might think. These priests, called Piaces in the islands, were much venerated, and even bigoted Spaniards resorted to them in times of anxiety. This superstition is not yet dead, nor, I suppose, will it ever die.

That the sculpture of the Chontals was of a school very different to that of the other races, is evident at a glance. The plain-dwelling people represented their gods as grotesque monsters, with awful eyes and malignant countenances, as did the mountaineers; but those simple and natural statues with which the Chontals piously adorned the cairns of their forefathers have no counterpart on the lower land. These figures would seem to indicate that the religion of the Chontals included some worship or veneration of ancestors, even though the main points of their creed might be identical with the Mexican. Such was the impression our discoveries left on the mind; but I should warn the reader that there is no historical authority for this belief. Many of the idols we discovered, both in Chontales and on the islands of the lake, had a hole drilled through them, in the head or the neck or the pedestal. In the colossal fragment figured on page 242 this was especially noticeable. A channel of two inches diameter passed quite through the throat, and out at the back of the neck. The theory one would naturally form would connect these holes with the bloody sacrifices offered in the old times before these idols, and in confirmation of this view, Peter Martyr observes, in Dec. III. lib. i.—" Here they offer to their gods the blood of children, pouring it through a hole in the neck." This occurs in his account of the southern islands, where was also practised the sacrifice of blood drawn from the tongue. It seems probable that this pouring of blood through the statue was used in Nicaragua also.

After the massacre of the Nicaraguan Rangers at the close of the "filibuster war," two survivors, Captain P—— and another, were concealed by a brave miner of Libertad, whose name I shall often have occasion to mention. When their wounds were healed, this gentleman, unwilling to desert men whom he had so boldly sheltered, procured a canoe, and embarked with them on the Rio Mico, which flows past Libertad through the Mosquito country to Blewfields. In this long voyage, through a region untrodden by Europeans since the days of Drake, they observed extraordinary remains of antique civilization. One scene in especial has strangely impressed the fancy of these reckless men. For some time the river had been gradually narrowing, and at length, one evening, they found themselves between vine-draped cliffs, so lofty that the sky was narrowed to a riband. Awestruck and silent they floated downwards. Suddenly the great walls receded as if by a landslip, and on the left, clear-lined against the sunset sky, stood a giant group of figures, that seemed on guard before the awful gap. The spectacle was so grand and solemn that they rested long on their paddles, gazing upwards. No eye but that of the barbarous Woolwa, or the not less savage Rama, had ever seen that sight. The figures were those of animals, carved in all postures. A solid cliff had been hewn down to leave them in this solitary grandeur. Erect they stood on that lonely precipice, eternal monuments of their builders' power.*

Wonderful indeed is the prospect which Central America offers to the antiquary. " Beside the stone enigmas of Palenque and Copan, the mysterious romance of the Itzimaya—the true story of which is by no means so absurd as we are used to believe in England—besides the treasures that lie buried on the Chiriqui, there are, if we may believe report, dead cities of far greater size and splendour than any yet known.

* Most conspicuous among these animals was a colossal bear, an animal unknown in Central America. We several times met with the representation of a beast exceedingly like a bear, both in Chontales and on the plains. Peter Martyr says, that in the islands—where the animal is equally unknown—" many images of bears were found sculptured in stone and marble."—Cozumella, Dec. III. lib. i.

In the wild Mosquito territory are vast remains of a civilization long since passed away. Sometimes, on the lonely shores of the Mico, amidst the unstayed vegetation of a thousand years, the startled traveller is brought face to face with works of such magnitude, sculptures of such colossal boldness, as tell him of a perished race as far superior to that the Spaniards found as the builders of Thebes to the Nile 'fellaheen.' He sees rocks cut down to the shape of men and animals; artificial hills encased in masonry; streams turned from their courses; volumes of hieroglyphics sculptured upon every cliff. Or, turning to the southward, there, across the San Juan river, dwells that mysterious and dreaded people the Guatusos, or white Indians of the Rio Frio. This strange and indomitable race, who may possibly owe their bravery and love of freedom to an ancestry of English buccaneers, occupy the north-east corner of Costa Rica; and there, surrounded by settled country, within three weeks of direct course from England, they positively keep the wealthiest district of that republic as completely closed to the world as if it were sunk beneath the Atlantic. What stories have we not heard of them from Caribs and Indians? What tales of wonder are too wild for belief when they relate to the country of the dreadful Guatusos?"*

* From a Paper read by the Author before the Archæological Institute. A few days before we sailed from Greytown, news reached the consul there of the discovery of a mighty city near Blewfields. What a glow one feels in dreaming of a life spent in the solution of these problems! "One sight of the Itzimaya," says Mr. Stevens, "would be worth ten years of ordinary life." I think it would almost be worth life itself.

END OF VOL. I.

www.ingramcontent.com/pod-product-compliance
Lightning Source LLC
Chambersburg PA
CBHW030011240426

43672CB00007B/906